ADVANCE PRAISE

"I have always deeply enjoyed talking and listening to Bob Moesta. He makes you think about things, differently with a compelling logic. In Learning to Build, there is much that you will nod your head and agree with while smiling at how well it is described till you're hit with a left hook that you never saw coming.

In a very productive way, he knocked me out of my conventional view of things and gave me insights on how to be more systematic in creating entrepreneurs and innovators. I love this kind of systematic approach to improving our ability to innovate, and I highly recommend this to ALL entrepreneurs to help them know good habits from bad. Go ahead and take the red pill—you won't regret it."

—**Bill Aulet**, Professor of Entrepreneurship at MIT Sloan School of Management, Managing Director of the Martin Trust Center for MIT Entrepreneurship, and author of *Disciplined Entrepreneurship*

"New product innovation is the only real growth engine for a business since all of its existing offerings and capabilities are built into the current value. But innovation is often a very risky business and doesn't always turn out the way we expect it.

Innovation doesn't have to be a crapshoot. There are tools to make innovation more predictable and successful. In this book, Bob combines science and practice into a playbook on how to do innovation right and build products that customers will find useful and are willing to pay for.

All of the five skills in this book are learnable and, together, are one of the best frameworks that I have seen for creating magical products. In particular, Bob masterfully explains the Uncovering Demand skill, which is probably the most critical part of an innovator's journey. I wish I had known about these when I was in my twenties."

—**Moe Tanabian**, Vice President at Microsoft AI

"People believe innovation is some magic reserved for a select few companies and individuals. In reality, innovation is an ability that can be learned and mastered. Bob taught me many of the necessary skills over a decade ago, and through this book, he can teach you, too."

—**Jon Lax**, Vice President of Design AR/VR at Facebook

"Bob is one of the industry's masters. In Learning to Build, he distills years of experience into a practical guide toward building those skills essential to innovation. It's a must-read for entrepreneurs, business owners, and all those seeking to innovate in their lives and work."

—**Max Wessel**, Executive Vice President and
Chief Learning Officer at SAP

"Through well-researched content, personal anecdotes, and reflection on his own experience as an innovator, Bob reveals the skills required for success. This book is vital for those who want to master innovation."

—**Terry Waters**, CEO of Devada, Inc

"Organized around five critical skills—and the valued mentors who influenced his thinking—Learning to Build is perfect for entrepreneurs, business owners, and anyone else hoping to acquire the skills necessary for innovation."

—**Todd Rose**, Co-founder/President of Populace and
author of *Dark Horse and The End of Average*

"It is a great thing for the world that Bob the builder is increasingly Bob the teacher. There are many books on innovation methods and tools. While this unique book includes those, it is more about what he refers to as 'the stuff in between.' Innovation methods and tools are like bricks in a foundation—but bricks don't work well without mortar in between them. Learning to Build provides mortar that firms and strengthens as you practice the five skills of an innovator in your life and work."

—**Jay Gerhart**, Vice President of Innovation Engine at Atrium Health

"Regardless of your profession, having a strong set of thinking tools is the difference between status quo and consistent progress. This book brings to life the critical skills of innovation that aren't taught in school and are often drowned out in a sea of buzzwords. Through personal experience and reflection on the wisdom of his mentors, Bob offers advice on how you can put these skills into practice in your work."

—**Andy Weisbecker**, Senior Director of Digital Experience at Target Corporation

"I couldn't put this book down. The amount of practical learning per page is phenomenal. Bob takes his personal story and learnings to explain the foundation of what it takes to be a successful innovator like no one else has—and shatters several myths of 'the best' ways to innovate in the process."

—**Michael Horn**, author of *Choosing College* and *Disrupting Class*

LEARNING TO BUILD

LEARNING TO BUILD

THE *5* BEDROCK SKILLS OF INNOVATORS AND ENTREPRENEURS

BOB MOESTA

LIONCREST
PUBLISHING

LEARNING TO BUILD

The 5 Bedrock Skills of Innovators and Entrepreneurs

ISBN	978-1-5445-2400-9	*Hardcover*
	978-1-5445-2398-9	*Paperback*
	978-1-5445-2399-6	*Ebook*
	978-1-5445-2401-6	*Audiobook*

To my mentors: Drs. Clayton Christensen, Genichi Taguchi,
W. Edwards Deming, and Willie Hobbs Moore, who shared
their knowledge with me so that I could pay it forward.

CONTENTS

FOREWORD

By Des Traynor, Co-Founder
and Chief Strategy Officer, Intercom

"*What's the next big opportunity?*" is the most common question you hear in businesses of all shapes and sizes. I've heard it from fresh faced startup founders on day one and from tenured CEOs on day one thousand. I often try to reframe the question for them; the important question is "*How do we consistently find the next big opportunity,*" and that's a question I can only answer because of one man: Bob Moesta.

I still remember where I was when I finally found out who Bob was. I had spent weeks, potentially months, chasing down who was the mysterious character that connected all the dots between researching milkshakes, moving houses, and new methodologies I'd never heard of.

Once I had his details, shared with me by a friend, I immediately emailed him. The startup world needed to hear about Bob Moesta, and more than that, I did. We had a successful startup, and our primary question was simply "Where do we go from here?" That proved to be a great question for someone like Bob.

We spoke for over two hours about innovation. He introduced me to new concepts like what it means to innovate on the demand side, why there are no sales professors, and how to identify struggling moments in customers' lives, and he taught me to focus purely on the causal relationships in our business. In a data-rich world of endless, weak correlations and flakey A/B tests, Bob's voice was important, if isolated: talk to your users and look for the chain of events. He taught me to find innovations in the connected series of small clues drawn from deep customer interviews, not from simple seven-point surveys sent to thousands. Jeff Bezos recently remarked, "When the anecdotes and the data disagree, the anecdotes are usually right." I suspect he would get along with Bob.

Bob is a builder, a successful one, and unlike many, he has an incredible ability to articulate his process. This is because Bob is a teacher, a successful one, and unlike many, he has built many successful businesses and advised hundreds more. This book will guide you through the important invariants in Bob's approach to building, and when you're finished, you'll start seeing new opportunities everywhere in your business.

When you finally put this book down, you'll no longer struggle to find areas to innovate in your business. You'll have a new and much better problem based on the wealth of opportunities you now see: where to start?

PART ONE

SETTING THE SCENE

INTRODUCTION

"After this, there is no turning back. You take the blue pill—the story ends, you wake up in your bed and believe whatever you want to believe. You take the red pill—you stay in Wonderland, and I show you how deep the rabbit-hole goes."

—**Morpheus**, fictional character, *The Matrix*

BLUE PILL	RED PILL
BACK TO MORE OF THE SAME	OPEN TO THE POSSIBILITY
SUPPLY–SIDE ORIENTED	DEMAND–SIDE ORIENTED
PLANNING THE KNOWNS	FOCUSING ON UNKNOWNS
MANAGEMENT OF THE GAPS	QUESTIONING, LEARNING + EMPIRICAL
TECHNOLOGY LED	ACCOUNTING FOR VARIATIONS
PROCESS FOCUSED	DESIGNING FOR THE REAL WORLD – NOISE
TIME + MONEY MANAGEMENT	EMPIRICAL EXPERIMENTS + BUILD THEORY
THEORY BASED – KNOWN	EMERGENT, EVER CHANGING AND PROGRESS
PUSH TO THE MARKET	PULL FOCUSED

Be prepared; this book is the red pill of innovation. You can never unsee what I'm going to reveal. The real world of innovation is not what it seems and certainly not what I'd been taught in school...

My story of unraveling *The Matrix* began the summer of my junior year in college when I had the opportunity to do an engineering internship at a major car manufacturer about developing and launching new products. At the time in 1985, the manufacturer was launching a new version of a popular car line, and they'd discovered a problem: 43 percent of the newly designed rearview mirrors would pop out of their holder when the weather got too hot and humid.

The key culprit seemed to be the polymer case holding the mirror; it was sensitive to swings in the ambient temperature. The problem started during the manufacturing of the cases. The polymer base would trap moisture from the surrounding environment of the plant when it was being molded, and then when the temperatures got too hot, this would cause the case to expand too much, and the mirrors would drop out. You'd get into the car, go to start the engine, look up, and the mirror would be missing; it was sitting on the dashboard. A simple solution would have been a more expensive polymer or an adhesive, but the manufacturer did not want to spend the extra money.

By the time the manufacturer had discovered the problem, cars were already on the assembly line and in the customer's hands; now they were getting warranty claims. When my internship started, the engineers had been working on the issue for a few months without any real success, so they decided to use it as a case study for the interns. My job, as I saw it, was to identify the problem and find the solution—simple enough.

Immediately, I started looking at the problem in terms of the exception to the rule: what was different in the 40 percent of cars where this anomaly occurred?

The Atlanta plant was having a significant problem because of the humid climate. Could we air condition the plant? No. Doing this would increase the costs significantly, negating the manufacturer's original purpose of cost savings.

Next, I toured the plant manufacturing the mirrors. They had a huge injection molding machine the size of a half-ton truck that melted plastic pellets and cast them into molds. Then the mirrors came out of the machine sixteen at a time, were hand inspected, trimmed for flash, and hit the assembly line where they were popped into their cases by workers on the production line. I realized that the mirrors were popped into their cases while they were still warm. So I suggested a longer drying process, but this created assembly line issues and again increased costs.

There was a lot of back and forth on my part, a lot of trial and error.

Finally, I thought I had a solution. I adjusted the chemical composition of the plastic so the case stopped changing so much in the face of the moisture. Eureka! It seemed that I had a solution. Right away, the mirrors stopped popping out of their cases in the humidity. My success was short lived; now, when the weather got too cold, the mirrors contracted and cracked the glass lens.

Why couldn't I solve this problem? What was I doing wrong? This was way different than what I was learning at school where every problem had one unique and exact answer.

It seemed every new solution created a new problem or added a new procedure that made the price skyrocket. I was chasing my tail. Each time I solved one problem, I caused another. Every time I felt like I'd made progress, I realized *Oh my God. I've traded one problem for another*. It always felt like I was one prototype away from the answer, yet I never got any closer to solving the problem.

My problem was unclear to me at the time; the training I relied on hampered any real progress.

What's the Difference Between an Inventor and an Innovator?

An inventor discovers something completely new. It's patentable. It solves one problem for one person. An inventor creates something that has never been done before. Inventors tend to be academically smart, and they value the uniqueness of their idea above all else. But they usually have no idea how their invention is going to help anybody. A Segway is a good example of an invention. It's a completely new idea, but it hasn't been widely adopted or accepted because it doesn't solve a problem on a large scale.

An innovator, on the other hand, focuses on society as a whole, looking for ways to help people do better. An innovator says, "I know there are tons of email programs, but I'm going to build a better one because the existing programs suck for these reasons…" Innovators want to help people be unstuck. The iPhone is a good example of an innovation. If you think about it, nothing in the iPhone was new to the world of technology, but it fundamentally changed the world. It's been adopted by hundreds of millions of people.

Whether you're an entrepreneur, a software developer, or somebody who likes to tinker, innovation is the notion of solving a struggling moment and helping people at scale.

MY REAL EDUCATION BEGAN

It's at this pivotal moment that I was introduced to an entirely new worldview of problem-solving by three key innovators hired by the car giant to get to the root of several manufacturing problems.

Leading the effort was my boss, Dr. Willie Moore—an engineer from the University of Michigan and the first female African American particle physicist. Alongside her were two outside consultants: Dr. W. Edwards Deming—quality guru and statistician—and Dr. Genichi Taguchi—Japanese engineer and father of quality engineering methods. I was the intern who was like a fly on the wall, soaking it all in. Little did I know at the time that their combined mentorship would become a catalyst for my life's work in innovation, new product development, and entrepreneurism.

"Looking at and focusing on problems is the wrong view of the world," Taguchi would say. He reminded me of Mr. Miyagi from the *Karate Kid* in the 1980s. "All problems are really problems about the variation of function: focus on what it's supposed to do, not what it's *not* supposed to do. There are infinite problems and only finite functions."

Taguchi told me that I needed to look at the issue differently. Instead of focusing on the problem or the symptom, I should have been looking at the function of the mirror case—the structure— and the variation of function that caused the problem: how the structure changed in the face of temperature, humidity, and time. I was struggling to find a solution because I was focused on only one of the problems—the mirror case becoming too loose. By focusing on that, I only saw half the issue, and I did not think about the other problems my solution could cause—the mirror could crack.

"There are always two sides of a problem, never one," Taguchi told me.

I needed to change my perspective, take a step back, and look at the situation more broadly. How could we make cases for the mirrors that would not expand and shrink in different temperatures and humidity? How could we build a case that was stable in extremely different climates? How could we make the mirror case dimensions "robust" to the environment it was going to perform in?

Rather than frame the problem and search for the solution like a needle in a haystack, I needed to look at the problem as a system with functions. What were the systems in the mirror case that were not performing the way that they should've? Then I needed to unpack those systems into control factors and noise factors.

- Control factors are parameters of a system you can change that impact the system's performance, and that you have the ability, responsibility, and control to set. In the manufacturing of our mirror case, we could change machine settings— injection pressure, barrel temperature, screw speed, hold time, etc.—and measure the dimensions molded against different temperatures and climates.

- Noise factors are the parameters that impact the system that you cannot control, you choose not to control, or that are too expensive to control. We did not have control over the humidity inside the plants or on the roads where the cars would be eventually driven. By only talking about this limited view of the "problem," a.k.a. the humidity, we were focused on something we could neither control nor change.

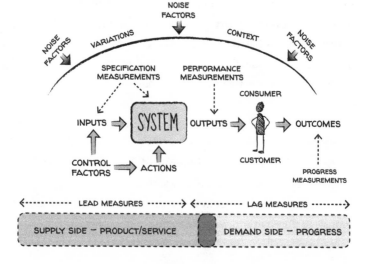

We needed to ask ourselves the following questions:

- How can we change the things that we have control over, control factors, to make us less sensitive to the things we cannot control, noise factors? (Taguchi defined this as robustness.)

- How do we set the control factors so that the noise factors no longer affect the output and get us the low-cost solution?

Once we answered these questions, we designed a set of experiments and tested only the things that were in our control—injection pressure, barrel temperature, screw speed, hold time, etc. But we did not test one factor at a time; we used an orthogonal array (math) to create a unique small set of prototypes that would explore thousands of combinations through only a few dozen tests at strategically different points. (Yes, I learned design of experiments for prototyping at nineteen.) We did not try to guess or build a great case; we let the math work for us and enabled the system to teach us what factors affected dimensional stability. Then we measured how the adjustments impacted the way that the cases were influenced by their environment.

After just two weeks, we solved the problem that had eluded the experts for over a year, reduced costs by 12 percent, and increased productivity—the trifecta. Dr. Taguchi taught me very early on that I didn't know the answer; therefore, I needed to test an array of combinations with data and let the "case" teach me about the best "case"—empirical, not theoretical. I loved it and dove in headfirst.

Over time, I realized that I'd been taught a very antiquated way to solve problems. In engineering school, they call them problem sets; everything is a problem. And you are always just one prototype or test away from solving the problem. When I finally got to work with real innovators, they taught me that it's not just one problem;

it's many problems which relate to a function and many different solutions that require you to make tradeoffs. By only framing the problem, we usually just framed the symptom and a way to measure it. We didn't actually understand the underlying causal mechanism of the bigger picture.

RETURNING TO SCHOOL

Going back to school was hard after learning this lesson from the dream team. Here I was a junior in college who had just learned all these new problem-solving techniques, and then I returned to school where they pushed me to think like all of the other engineers.

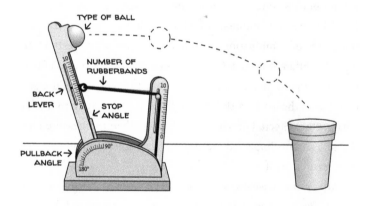

Almost immediately, I was asked to solve a problem with a catapult, rubber band, ball, and cup. "How many degrees do you need to pull back this rubber band to make the ball fly ten feet away and land in the cup?" my professor asked.

It was a basic question with a simple solution, but I no longer saw it that way. I imagined the catapult in the real world. What happens when the ball size changes? What about wind resistance? What about when the rubber band stretches over time? How does the catapult height figure into the equation? How does cup size factor in? I needed to design a set of experiments to understand how it really worked.

My professor had provided one problem and wanted the solution—the pull-back angle. Academically, I knew what he was trying to do, but I wanted to make the best, most robust, lowest cost catapult. I wanted to know how it worked in the real world and then optimize it.

So, I designed a simple set of nine experiments to test a variety of different parameters at different levels. I picked the most effective of the nine designs and presented my solution to the class. (You'll learn more about this approach in Chapter 6.)

I discovered that if I doubled the number of rubber bands, made the catapult shorter, and pulled the rubber band thirty-two degrees, my ball would land in the cup with 97 percent accuracy. Whereas the standard solution—twenty-two degrees—that my professor expected, the "right" answer, only landed the ball in the cup 57 percent of the time.

"No, no, no!" my professor said to me. "You are making it too complicated." In the end, I received a D for failing to follow the instructions.

They wanted me to frame the problem, think about the problem, and design a solution around the problem. They wanted me to do traditional A/B type testing where you create a hypothesis, test that hypothesis, and verify your hypothesis—the scientific method. Yet now I knew that there was another way forward, and I could not unsee it.

Under the leadership of Taguchi, Deming, and Moore, I had learned to assume that I knew nothing, test a set of different factors simultaneously to understand how the system worked, and only then to form a hypothesis, empirically through data and observation. When you realize that you do not know, it causes you to look at the system as interdependent and create a test that considers a bunch of different factors simultaneously. It's about taking a step back and seeing the big picture.

The traditional problem-solving techniques being taught when I went to school were not only inefficient and ineffective, but they were also putting blinders on me. I could only see the problem, be the problem, solve the problem. I was looking for the solution like a needle in a haystack. And then, "Oh, shit! I've got another problem."

I no longer wanted to focus on the problem. I wanted to know: what is it *supposed to do*?

APPLYING THE NEW METHODOLOGY

The next summer, I was pleased to escape the confines of the classroom and return to the same internship program and leadership team where I'd be able to apply these new problem-solving techniques.

I sat in the back of a conference room, side by side with Taguchi and Moore—a surreal moment in time as a young, curious student surrounded by intellectual heavyweights—facing another production-line dilemma. The car manufacturer was just beginning to use robots rather than people to paint cars, and they'd run into a problem. At the time, the robots that they were using to paint the cars weren't capable of applying the paint in a uniform way.

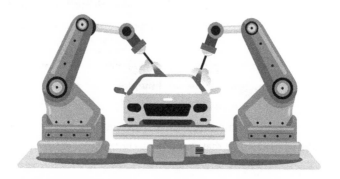

The system worked by taking the paint down the arm of the robot where it hit a spinning wheel that sprayed droplets over the vehicle. The droplets were positively charged with high voltage, and the cars had a negative charge. This caused the paint to be attracted to the vehicle. But as the droplets hit the surface of the vehicle, certain areas, depending on whether they were horizontal or vertical, would have drips; the paint was too thick. And when the experts adjusted the thickness of the paint, it resulted in an orange peel effect, because now the paint was too thin.

There was a lot of back and forth and prototyping, but no solution to the problem had been found. It caused significant rework, which was costing the manufacturer over $100 million annually at one plant.

Sitting in a room full of experts, I was acutely aware that I probably understood the least about paint systems of anyone, so I sat and listened. They talked at length about the laborious process they'd gone through to solve the issue, addressing factors such as humidity, paint color, and direction (horizontal versus vertical surfaces). They were focused on the problems—orange peel and runs—and how to reduce them. But they were trying to control the noise factors that were really out of their control: humidity, paint color, and direction. Taguchi leaned over to me and said, "They are measuring the wrong things. It's about the function—what it's supposed to do and reducing the variation, not the problems." I could see it clearly this time; we needed to flip the lens.

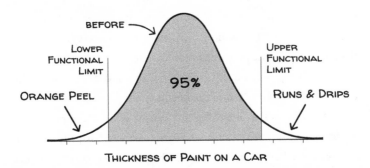

THICKNESS OF PAINT ON A CAR

"This is your project. We need you to see if you can reduce the rework," Taguchi said. Finally, my chance!

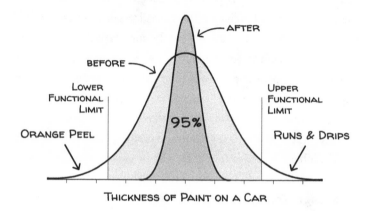

THICKNESS OF PAINT ON A CAR

Immediately, I got to work framing the issue differently. I took a step back and looked at the fundamentals. How did the system work? What function was it supposed to do? Turns out paint thickness is a way better measure: too thin, orange peel; too thick, runs. What was the variation that was causing the problems? How could I design a test to control the things I could control and see the robustness of the system in the face of the noise factors?

We needed a paint system that would cover the surface of cars evenly, regardless of the noise factors like operator, humidity, color, or direction. Therefore, I looked at the control factors: underlying base paint, paint thickness, spinning speed of the internal bell, speed of the robot arm, charge on the car, charge on the paint, and a few other parameters. In essence, I looked at the entire system rather than focusing on the presumed problem: orange peel and runs.

By focusing only on the problems (drips and orange peel), the experts were - trying to find the needle in the haystack. But I wondered: what was the one thing that caused all of these problems? Additionally, they talked about the orange peel and drips as two separate issues, whereas Taguchi had taught me to see them as two sides of the same function—paint thickness. They never talked about them as the same problem. They simply said, "What's the problem that we're trying to solve? What are the root causes to it?"

Conversely, I asked a different set of questions: What was it supposed to be doing? Where was the variation? What was causing it? How could I make myself least sensitive to the things I couldn't control?

Similar to the rearview mirror, I designed a small focus set of experiments that analyzed a variety of factors in painting a complex test piece; I never painted an entire car. Ultimately, I created eighteen focus tests that represented thousands of permutations which ran over a weekend. Quickly, I learned some of the better settings for reducing the variation of paint thickness, thus reducing both orange peel and runs at the same time. Meanwhile, the engineering team, singularly focused on one problem at a time, would cautiously change one factor at a time and paint a whole car. By only testing one factor at a time and painting an entire car, they approached the problem too carefully. After all, they had a lot more to lose each time their experiment failed. I, on the other hand, felt free to test more factors and explore the unknowns.

But when I came back and showed them my results, they balked. "You can't do that; that's not how the math works. You'd have to test all five thousand combinations to find the best one." So I showed them what Taguchi, Deming, and Moore had taught me.

"I'm doing these eighteen tests, but they're spaced out in such a way that I can actually predict what the other test results would be," I explained. I knew I was not necessarily getting the perfect run, but it got us in the top 90 percent.

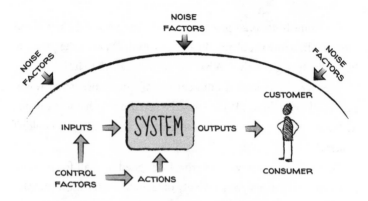

The reason that I was able to quickly solve the problem that had eluded the engineers for the past year was not because I was the smartest person in the room, but because I viewed the problem from a different perspective. It felt like Taguchi, Deming, and Moore had given me a superpower; I'd swallowed the red pill and now I could dodge virtual bullets.

THE FIVE SKILLS OF INNOVATORS AND ENTREPRENEURS

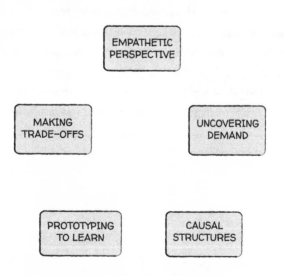

Throughout my more-than-thirty-year career developing and launching over thirty-five hundred products and services, I've come across thousands of other innovators and entrepreneurs. The top ten stand out to me, just as my key mentors stood out. One day, I intentionally took a step back and asked myself, *What do these people think or do differently from others? What skills do they possess?* Upon reflection, I narrowed it down to five subtle skills that set them apart. These are the hidden parts of innovation that nobody seems to teach in an in-depth way—the stuff in between innovation tools and processes—and I believe that they are the things that differentiate successful innovators and entrepreneurs I've met along the way from being typical engineers, software developers, or CEOs.

 Empathetic Perspective: people with this skill can detach from their own perspective and see the subtle differences between the many different perspectives surrounding their thing—internally and externally.

 Uncovering Demand: people with this skill can detach from their product or service and look at the demand-side of the equation—seeing struggles, context, and outcomes.

 Causal Structures: people with this skill have a dominant view of how the world works based in cause and effect.

Prototyping to Learn: people with this skill know that they do not have all the answers and run tests to get empirical data to discover and build new theory instead of relying on existing theory and testing hypotheses.

Making Tradeoffs: people with this skill understand that they cannot do everything and are skilled at making essential tradeoffs to launch a product that is not perfect.

The goal of this book is to take an in-depth look at these five skills and why they are so important. On the surface, they feel like concepts that you already grasp. It's true the ideas presented in this book are not new. For instance, I'm sure you've heard that having an empathetic perspective is important when innovating. But like *The Matrix*, what you think you know and what you know are two different things. You need to be humble enough to realize that there's way more here than you recognize.

By calling out these five skills, I want to impart the importance of the role that they play; it's the rigor and depth behind them that I wish to convey. Most people perform these five skills too shallowly. And those who do understand the importance of their depth didn't acquire that knowledge in a classroom or a book. They did so through life experiences. My hope is to pave an easier path for you by making them explicit and giving you a way to see and practice them.

I also want to pay homage to my key mentors Taguchi, Deming, and Moore, as well as another great, Clay Christiansen of the

Harvard Business School, with whom I architected a theory called "Jobs to Be Done" (JTBD). It's the notion that people don't buy products; they hire them to make progress in their life. It gets to the root of supply versus demand. All four of these innovation giants shaped me. I was a receptacle for their knowledge; it became a part of me, and I want to pass their wisdom along to whomever wants to listen.

However, this book isn't a roadmap that will dictate the *only* true way to innovate; it's about putting more arrows in your quiver rather than debating the "best" way to innovate. It's simply a collection of the lessons and tools that I learned along the way, the things that helped me make progress. In reality, there might be a hundred different ways to effectively innovate, and it depends on your context. It's up to you to decide which elements to pick and choose. And like anything else, I expect the wisdom shared in this book will someday become obsolete. But everything new is built on the old, so I felt it was my responsibility to share with you what was shared with me in hopes of advancing the innovations of tomorrow.

In a lot of ways, innovation and entrepreneurship are like riding a bike. Individually, the pieces seem simple: balance, steering, pedaling, brakes, and so on. You theoretically understand how to do it. You study it first, but putting those theories into practice is an entirely different thing. If you don't nail balance, the rest of it doesn't work. And the first time that you try to pull it all together, you find that it's way more complex than you expected; you don't want to fall and hit the ground.

The five skills of innovators and entrepreneurs that are taught in this book are the things that helped me get past those first moments of panic; they gave me an approach and guardrails for building and creating and allowed me to adapt. Now I have little fear. When I walk into a situation, I'm humble enough to know that I don't have the answers, but these five skills provide me the confidence to know that I will discover the answer.

Today, I am in my seventh startup—The Re-Wired Group—with my partner and co-founder Greg Engle. Greg and I have worked on developing and launching products together for more than seventeen years. At Re-Wired, we provide consulting and design services that help companies develop and launch new products. Greg and I work side by side with our clients to help them understand buyer behaviors and build better products. These five skills are what our clients call the "Re-Wired Magic."

ARE YOU STRUGGLING TO INNOVATE?

Someone recently told me that I reminded them of Doc Brown, the fictional character from *Back to the Future* who invents time travel. I hope that we have time travel at some point. How great would that be to go back in time and teach the younger version of ourselves the lifetime of wisdom that we learned along the way? This book is akin to that. It's the notion of passing it forward. Of showing you the world as it was seen through "young Bob's" eyes and how that world ultimately transformed into the innovator that "enlightened Bob" is today.

Does this sound familiar?

- Are you always one prototype away from a solution but never seem to get there?

- Do you spend most of your time fixing problems that you did not anticipate?

- Does it seem like everything is going well right up until launch when it all falls apart?

- Are you getting very little return on the resources you deploy?

- Does the performance of your product in the market rarely meet the predicted targets?

If you answered yes, then you are like young Bob. Let me teach you both the science and art to innovation. My hope for you is once you pull together the fundamental pieces, it will spin you up in a way that allows you to see the world nobody else can see—*The Matrix*—and building will become your superpower too.

CHAPTER ONE

WHAT'S AN INNOVATOR?

I know you want to dive right into the five skills of innovators and entrepreneurs, but first we need to gain a little more perspective and build some common ground on how new products are created. To do that, let's continue my journey back in time...

By 1988, now a graduate, I found myself working full-time at the car manufacturer, still under the direction of Taguchi, Deming, and Moore. Despite the establishment of many better problem-solving techniques, we still weren't keeping up with our Japanese competition and neither were our American counterparts. In Japan, industry leaders were creating new cars in half the time—three years from conception to release, compared to our six—and they were also doing this at half the cost, which was kind of amazing.

If we wanted to stay competitive in the industry, we'd need to make drastic changes, and fast. That's when Deming, a team of executives, and myself went to Japan on a study mission. After a careful analysis, we noticed significant differences between our development process and our Japanese counterparts. We came to refer to this as "red line" versus "green line" development.

Let's contrast the two approaches. On the red line, our process started with an early concept design that was readily accepted. The design would be committed to paper, where we would spell out the details—engine, transmission, body, etc. At this early stage, we'd make only slight modifications. Then each team would break off into their individual silos and begin working on their element.

The engine designer would make the best engine, the transmission designer built the ideal transmission, and so on. Agreement and common understanding were *assumed*, and the early process would run relatively smoothly—changes were in the thousands.

RED-LINE DEVELOPMENT

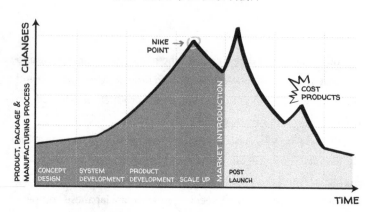

But as we got closer and closer to launch, design changes would skyrocket—by almost one hundred times. Our teams worked in silos that were extremely independent, so they never consulted one another in an in-depth or meaningful fashion as they built out their components. As a result, when we got close to launch and finally started to pull everything together, there would be problems; the car would not connect perfectly. For instance, we'd put the transmission and the engine together, then something would break.

From a cost perspective, discovering these conflicts and differences late is disastrous. Now it would take a massive effort and significant time and money to fix them. At the beginning of the design, changes are negligible; it's on paper only. On the backend, however, changes run in the millions. There are custom steel tools that now must be replaced, costing in the millions each. Plus, each change impacts another element, which then must also be adjusted.

COST OF MAKING DESIGN CHANGES

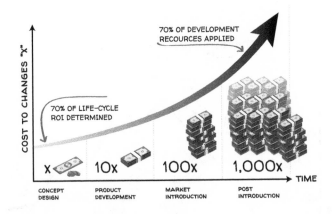

It felt like a high-stakes game of whack-a-mole, with a very real, looming deadline just around the corner. In the end, we would have to freeze the design and launch the car, then go back and patch up problems after launch—like the rearview mirror. The red line was a very reactive process!

When I laid out the graph of changes over time for our green line competition, I saw something quite different...

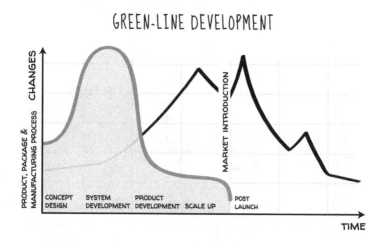

GREEN-LINE DEVELOPMENT

For starters, the Japanese manufacturer did not start with one readily accepted concept design. Instead, they had multiple prototypes and made tons of changes in the early stages when the design was still on paper—one hundred times the prototypes. Then when they eventually broke off into their individual silos, there was a lot of communication to ensure their components worked together and that they understood each other's perspectives. Nothing was assumed. In essence, they pushed their product to fail early in the process, before they ever pulled the entire design together, dramatically reducing time and money spent.

In the end, the Japanese manufacturer got to the finish line with a lot less drama. And oh, by the way, their cars actually performed better in the marketplace too. We needed to change our approach.

A DIFFERENT WAY TO INNOVATE

"I would not give a fig for the simplicity on this side of complexity, but I would give my life for the simplicity on the other side of complexity."

—**Oliver Wendell Holmes, Jr.,** Former Associate Justice of the Supreme Court

As a young engineer, I was beginning to realize that there was a behavioral side to successful innovation. It wasn't enough to simply know how to build; the approach to the process mattered too.

On the red line, our process was very prescribed, standardized; it removed thinking. We simply followed the process—it worked (or so we thought)—think "best practices." But we were planning (or guessing) when we were the stupidest; I call this simplicity on the wrong side of complexity. It's easy to develop the best engine if you don't need to consider the transmission. We only planned what we knew and never anticipated the unknowns or discovered tasks along the way.

The green line developers approached their process from a different perspective. They took a step back and viewed the whole, which caused them to do the right things at the right time. Rather than using their process to remove thinking, their process created the space for deeper thinking, collaboration, and continuous improvement. They not only made things work but also knew where they broke; their focus was on parallel development (versus serial), which caused them to use prototyping in a very different way. As a result, they had a deeper understanding of the customer that went beyond the customer's voice and what they stated to a place where they understood intent. We used pictures, while they used movies; we saw problems, whereas they saw systems; we watched and waited while they made it fail early and often to learn. In essence, we were arrogant, and they were humble. I found that overall, their approach was way more about mindset than just process.

This isn't just the story of two commercial car companies. It's the story of two development teams and their approach to the process of creating new things. Throughout my career I've found that most organizations create new products on the red line. What kind of company are you? Young Bob was a red line innovator, but I've evolved and so can you.

Through tens of thousands of hours of practice, and through interactions with some of the most influential innovators in the world, I've reflected on my experience with them and boiled down the difference between red line innovation and green line innovation into the five skills of innovators and entrepreneurs. They are the unwritten skills that I've developed over the years after first trying, failing, learning, and finally succeeding. Throughout the upcoming chapters, I will teach you how to build these critical skills, but first, let's take a brief look.

EMPATHETIC PERSPECTIVE

EMPATHETIC PERSPECTIVE

PEOPLE WITH THIS SKILL CAN DETACH FROM THEIR OWN PERSPECTIVE AND SEE THE SUBTLE DIFFERENCES BETWEEN THE MANY DIFFERENT PERSPECTIVES SURROUNDING THEIR THING—INTERNALLY AND EXTERNALLY

When you're on the red line, your own perspective is the most important one. If I'm the engine guy, I need to make sure that I explain my perspective to the person building the transmission, but I'm less sensitive to their perspective. I don't truly consider the transmission designer's point of view when building my design. I may imagine what they think, but that's vastly different than knowing; it's very superficial.

Whereas on the green line, I see the situation from multiple per-spectives: the customer buying the product, the designer develop-ing the transmission, the people on the assembly line, etc. I get out of the conference room or the engine lab and seek out their per-spective. I walk the assembly line, I talk to the transmission designer, and I utterly understand the many perspectives that could impact my system. Then when I go back to build, I do so with that in mind so that I can see the conflicts before they arise.

UNCOVERING DEMAND

UNCOVERING DEMAND
PEOPLE WITH THIS SKILL CAN DETACH FROM THEIR PRODUCT OR SERVICE AND LOOK AT THE DEMAND-SIDE OF THE EQUATION—SEEING STRUGGLES, CONTEXT, AND OUTCOMES.

When I was young and developing products on the red line, I was told to "build it, and people will come." Demand on the red line was the number of "people" in a certain age group and demographic set; I could have everybody. The target market was an amazingly simple notion—*who*. It was attributes and correlative demographics in a very superficial way.

But what causes someone to buy? The fact that I'm fifty-five, live in this zip code, and have that income does not cause me to buy the *New York Times*. Something happened that caused me to say, "Today's the day that I'm going to subscribe to the *New York Times*." What?

Green line innovators understand what *causes* people to buy or to change behavior. Specific things had to happen in my life before I said, "Today's the day…" Value is in the eye of the buyer, and uncov-ering demand is about understanding where your buyer's value is created. And to be clear, profit is not value; creating value for the company is different than creating value for the customer. Ultimately, uncovering demand is about broadening your worldview and realizing that innovation is about helping people. It's not about you or your product's features and benefits; it's about who, when, where, and why. This is the key to defining demand.

CAUSAL STRUCTURES

CAUSAL STRUCTURES
PEOPLE WITH THIS SKILL HAVE A DOMINANT VIEW OF HOW THE WORLD WORKS BASED IN CAUSE AND EFFECT.

On the red line, people tend to focus on problems and solutions. It's very reactionary. They wait for a problem to arise, then react. They focus myopically on one aspect or feature but fail to see the whole. People on the red line chase their tails like young Bob with the rearview mirror. Every solution creates another problem, and they are always one problem away from the answer, yet they never get any closer to a solution.

Whereas on the green line, people see the big picture and understand how the entire system works. People who are good at causal structures understand that a problem is a derivative of functions and variations of functions within a system. They are curious and develop a deep understanding of how things work—a broad, big picture view as opposed to a myopic, singularly focused view.

For example, think of the robot paint problem from the Introduction. When scientists focused on fixing orange peel, they got runs, and when they focused on runs, they got orange peel. Each solution created a new problem because they were working in the "problem space." When I eventually solved the problem, I did so primarily because I focused on the "function space"—thickness of paint. There are always two sides to every problem. People good at causal structures take a step back and see the whole.

PROTOTYPING TO LEARN

PROTOTYPING TO LEARN

PEOPLE WITH THIS SKILL KNOW THAT THEY DO NOT HAVE ALL THE ANSWERS AND RUN TESTS TO GET EMPIRICAL DATA TO DISCOVER AND BUILD NEW THEORY INSTEAD OF RELYING ON EXISTING THEORY AND TESTING HYPOTHESES.

On the red line, people do a lot of A/B testing. This is a direct result of looking at the world through the "problem space" as opposed to the "function space." Because they think in terms of one problem and one solution, they go looking for answers like a needle in a haystack. What's the one thing that will solve our problem? It's the notion of testing one factor at a time. Results on the red line are not typically reproducible because they are isolated, aimed at finding the "one" root cause that made the problem.

Whereas on the green line, because they are in the "function space," they design experiments that change many variables at once to learn how the system works, assuming nothing. They are prototyping to understand the possible ways it can fail. Constantly asking, "What are the failure modes?" This understanding allows them to reduce costs while solving problems because they can see the whole. They find the "root causes"—the sets of things that work together to make the system work.

On the green line, you're focused on learning. Whereas on the red line, you are testing to prove a hypothesis, to verify, and then when it doesn't work you point fingers at everyone else.

MAKING TRADEOFFS

MAKING TRADE-OFFS

PEOPLE WITH THIS SKILL UNDERSTAND THAT THEY CANNOT DO EVERYTHING AND ARE SKILLED AT MAKING ESSENTIAL TRADE-OFFS TO LAUNCH A PRODUCT THAT IS NOT PERFECT.

On the red line, people are not taking the time to see tradeoffs. Let's say for instance that you are creating a mobile app of a desktop application. If you try to do everything on the mobile app that's available on the desktop, the system will run slow. You can have it all, but you will lose functionality, or you can strip it back to only the pieces that people would use a mobile app for. It'll be faster but not fully functional.

On the red line, people are focused on making everything perfect, so they do not see the big picture and therefore can't make tradeoffs. They usually end up way over budget only to find that their product isn't that well received in the marketplace. Whereas on the green line, they can see the whole and understand where to make explicit tradeoffs. They have an eye on cost and demand, so the tradeoffs are easy.

You can probably already identify areas of strengths and weaknesses after those brief descriptions. Luckily, these skills are not innate; they can be learned. Before we dig deep into each, let's look at the green line development process from an individual perspective—that of a dear friend who's already mastered the five hidden skills of innovators and entrepreneurs.

THE MYTH ABOUT FAILURE AND INNOVATION

There's a mantra in the world of innovation that says, "If you're not failing, then you're not innovating." But failure by itself is not a rite of passage to becoming an innovator. It's the learning that comes from failing that makes someone an innovator.

If I leave a failure on the table without uncovering *why*, then it's a waste—making failure useful is the hard part of innovation. In my experience, great innovators are obsessed with understanding why their system failed; it's the opportunity to learn.

When I fail, I turn to the five skills taught in this book and ask myself, *What was I missing?* Then I get up and try again differently.

APPLYING THE FIVE SKILLS OF AN INNOVATOR

How does a product developer write a book?

My good friend Ryan—product strategist and developer at a software company—asked himself that question not too long ago. You see, his boss, a four-time *New York Times* bestselling author, had recently asked him to do just that—write a book about how their company develops products. By the time Ryan and I sat down for coffee later that week, his mind was spinning—too much and too little all at the same time.

"What the hell?" Ryan lamented. "I don't have any idea how to write a book! Every time I sit down to write, my mind locks up—so many unknowns. What am I going to do? What do people even want to know?" That was his turning point. Ryan realized that he simply needed to apply the same skills to writing a book as an innovator applies to developing software, and it all started with empathetic perspective and uncovering demand.

So the next day, Ryan created a basic invitation to a one-day, $1,000 workshop, billing it as a masterclass in product management techniques. "Announcement: Join me for a one-day workshop in Chicago, December 20th. 'Shape and Ship 1.0' is a workshop on Basecamp's product management techniques. Learn how we design, develop, and deliver new products and features. Apply by December 3rd."

He gave people five days to apply and created a list of hellacious essay questions that would get to the root of his question: what do people want to know?

Just five days later, Ryan had more than one hundred applicants. He chose twenty, a diverse twenty—those who articulated their struggles the best—and got to work creating the content. The class was just two weeks away. As he sat down to flush out the content, he realized that he had more than enough for a one-day workshop; he could've spent the entire week teaching.

The essay questions helped him along, but to completely understand his potential reader, the one-on-one interaction with other industry professionals would be critical. What "job" did they hire the workshop to do? After the class's conclusion, Ryan reached out to each of the twenty participants and conducted detailed interviews: where did they find value?

In the end, Ryan framed four "Jobs":

(1) HELP ME SHIFT RESPONSIBILITY   (2) HELP ME MAKE FASTER
    TO THE TEAM SO I CAN THINK   PROGRESS ON THE PRODUCT

| WHEN I AM | SO I CAN | | WHEN I AM | SO I CAN |
|---|---| |---|---|

(3) HELP ME BRING MY   (4) HELP ME PUT MY IDEAS
    TEAM ALONG   INTO A FORM THAT OTHER
                               PEOPLE CAN ACT ON

| WHEN I AM | SO I CAN | | WHEN I AM | SO I CAN |
|---|---| |---|---|

Armed with a good understanding of demand and empathetic perspective, Ryan created the structure of the book. Because Ryan now understood value from his customers' perspectives, he could step back, see the whole, and outline the book effectively—think systems and causal structures. Finally, he sat down to write. Now this time, rather than drawing a blank, the material flowed.

Shaping

Enemies to allies
- Betting

- Appetite →
- Fuel →
- Promising idea →

[System 1 — Sketching] → Promising concept → [System 2 — De-risking] → Shaped concept → [System 3 — Writing] → Potential bet → [System 4 — Betting] → Commitment
- Bet
- rebet
- Affirm

System 1 — Sketching
- Broadband sketches
- Clay on the table
- Fast
- Messy
- 2 people
- Trying different ideas

Fat marker
- "helicopter"
- Not wireframing
- "This is just an idea..."

System 2 — De-risking
- De-risking
- Dissolved drawings
- Rolled rules sheet
- Removing scope
- Fat marker
- Not wireframing
- engineer input
- Making the one idea work

System 3 — Writing
- "Write it up"
- Dissolved drawings
- Fat marker
- Accumulate
- 1) Problems
- 2) Communicate appetite
- Communicate what not to do
- Communicate motivation
- Selective hi-fi
- Not wireframing
- engineer input

→ Potential bet
- Stating
- Concept
- Public idea
- De-risk
- appetite

- Itinerary to bets

System 4 — Betting
- Reserve capacity & capability
- 6 weeks / 2 weeks
- Set expectation - entropy can interrupt
  - Do in and out
  - Do the work
  - The table & works
- Anything that owns up can be addressed as soon as 6 weeks from now
- Circuit breaker
- Designers + Programmers
- Big enough to matter
- Small enough arie not growing

Build — Take the hill

Step 5 — Kickoff
- 60–90 min call with team
- Q & A
- Red epicenters
- Expect to show work on
- Plan approach
- Velocity anxiety confidence
- Attempt to parallel work

Ground scope; getting thought

Step 6 — Spike
Get hands dirty sequence; updated tasks
- Real work
- Parallel work
- Betas errors
- Identify hidden dependencies
- Add tasks
  - Must chart
  - Maybe later (~)
- Start kill chart
- Figure out the natural boundaries
- Deploy continuously
- Learn by building
- Sense of urgency
- Feeling of risk
- Sense of accomplishment

Corrected scope; tasks

Step 7 — Chart uphill (on scope)
Mixtures of uphill, downhill, stuck, updated work
- Get most important scope out of "unknown"
- Pick one
- Estimate is waiting
- update kill chart
- Add must haves
- Check off tasks
- Add maybe later (~)
- Add extra scope
- Learn by building
- Deploy continuously
- Sense of urgency
- Feeling of risk
- Sense of accomplishment

updated sequence, revised scope, updated kill

Step 8 — Take stock
- Whats stuck?
- Whats most important
- updated kill chart
- Scope known
- How much time is left?
- Sense of urgency
- Feeling of risk

updated title; shipped, parts updated kill chart

Step — work (recap)
- Tasks done
- or
- update kill chart
- Scope known
- Deploy continuously
- Sense of urgency
- Feeling of risk
- Sense of accomplishment
- Mark scope complete

However, after finishing the book, he didn't immediately go on to find himself an editor or publisher; instead, he went in search of several businesses to apply the book. Did it make sense in practice? Was the language applicable across industry? Ryan was prototyping to learn, pushing his book to fail. Done, right? Nope.

Ryan then ran a second, two-day workshop. This was nine months after the first. This time, however, out of the many applicants, he chose twenty-five whose "Job" matched the material in the book. From there, he was able to further refine his content and finally publish. Phew! So how did the book perform?

Well, in true innovator fashion, Ryan used the process of disseminating the book to continue to prototype. You see, he did not publish the book in print. He set up a unique webpage that didn't even allow downloads so that he could watch people read the book in real time and see where they struggled.

Within three months, Ryan had almost 400,000 unique visitors to the book. After making his final changes, he finally made it available for download in a PDF format. As of September 2020, one year after its initial release, it was downloaded by 580,000 readers. Currently, he's launching the book in print format: *Shape Up: Stop Running in Circles and Ship Work that Matters*, by Ryan Singer.

Ryan took a step back, understood that he did not know, and used the five skills of innovators and entrepreneurs to make sense of the task of writing a book.

MAKING IT REAL

At this point, you may have an inkling of where you're already succeeding or failing with the five skills. Here's a set of questions to ask yourself:

- **Empathetic Perspective:** Do I deeply understand other people's perspectives—external customers and vendors, as well as internal designers and assembly line workers? Do I get where they are coming from? Can I play it all out through time?

- **Uncovering Demand:** Do I understand what *causes* demand for my product? What dominoes must fall before someone says, "Today's the day..." What *causes* someone to fire another product and hire mine?

- **Causal Structures:** Am I curious? Do I constantly want to figure out how things work, even when they're illogical or irrational? Do I believe in randomness? (Randomness is the opposite of causal structures.) Do I take the time to frame questions before building my prototypes?

- **Prototyping to Learn:** Am I building sets of prototypes, as opposed to prototyping two aspects at a time, A/B testing? Am I causing things to fail or waiting for them to fail and reacting?

- **Making Tradeoffs:** Am I striving for perfection, or can I see the whole and understand that I can't have everything? Do I understand how to frame my tradeoffs from both the supply-side and the demand-side? Do I err on the side of the customer or the company?

Throughout the next five chapters, I will delve deeply into each of the five skills of innovators and entrepreneurs and offer tools and techniques for you to practice in your own life. If you've read my book *Demand-Side Sales 101*, which was written and framed around how people buy, you will see some similarities, especially as it relates to empathetic perspective and uncovering demand. It's true there are similarities, but there are also subtle differences.

Ultimately, this book is about learning to manage and create things as opposed to just helping people buy, and as you will see, when the context changes, so does the meaning behind the tools. That said, let's start with empathetic perspective.

PART TWO

THE FIVE SKILLS

CHAPTER TWO

EMPATHETIC PERSPECTIVE

"A leader is a coach, not a judge."

—Dr. W. Edwards Deming

Imagine you're planning a long car trip with your spouse and children. Before you leave, you start to think through the steps involved in getting from point A to point B with the least resistance: How often will the kids need to stop for the restroom? Where are the restrooms? When and where will you stop for lunch? If you pick the one place that you and your spouse want to eat, the kids may mutiny. How many hours can the kids be in the car without too much difficulty? What will you bring to entertain them?

As you think about the trip, you imagine each of your kids and your spouse from their perspective. Then you figure out how to avoid conflicts as you play it out over space and time. This is empathetic perspective.

Empathetic perspective encapsulates the notion that there's not just the external customer perspective—demand-side—and the internal company perspective—supply-side—but there are many different perspectives within both supply and demand. The most successful innovators can see the subtle differences between the many different perspectives, which enables them to foresee problems and make tradeoffs. In many ways, people skilled at empathetic perspective have night vision goggles: they can *see around corners* and *see through space and time.*

- *Seeing around corners* happens when you have a 720-degree perspective (backwards, forwards, as well we up and down—three dimensional) of everyone interacting with your creation; it's all-encompassing, almost omniscient.

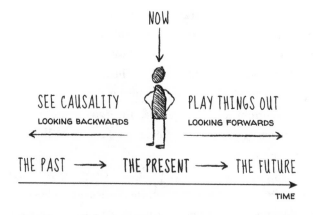

$$360° + 360° = 720°$$

- *Seeing through space and time* is about placing yourself in another person's shoes, which allows you to play out events before they've occurred and therefore anticipate disconnects, tradeoffs, and potential problems.

NOW

SEE CAUSALITY   PLAY THINGS OUT
LOOKING BACKWARDS   LOOKING FORWARDS

THE PAST ⟶ THE PRESENT ⟶ THE FUTURE

TIME

Let's create some contrast to create meaning. Think sympathy versus empathy: empathy is the ability to understand and internalize the feelings of another (think of it as playing a role in a play), whereas sympathy is your ability to relate to the feelings of another person. When you sympathize with someone, you're not putting yourself in the other person's shoes, feeling what they feel, seeing what they see.

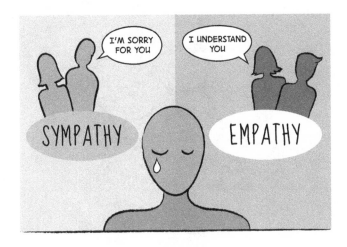

Innovators and entrepreneurs skilled at empathetic perspective have the ability to disconnect or mute from their own perspective—emotionally and socially—and see, hear, listen, and feel from another's point of view without judgment. You're not trying to convince your kid that they shouldn't need so many rest stops; you're not arguing about McDonald's versus Cracker Barrel. You're accepting their perspective without judgment and planning the trip, making tradeoffs along the way.

Think of planning a road trip in the example above as level one of empathetic perspective. Innovators and entrepreneurs, however, need to take this skill to the next level to be successful; it's about rigor and depth.

UNDERSTANDING EXTERNAL CUSTOMERS THROUGH EMPATHETIC PERSPECTIVE

Currently, I'm helping to teach a class with Professor Ethan Bernstein at Harvard Business School about managing human capital. What *causes* people to change jobs or make progress in their career? How do you manage people better so that you retain them? How do you attract the best people to your organization?

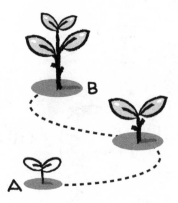

Answering these questions starts with empathetic perspective—learning to see things from other's perspectives without being emotionally connected. And to do that, you must listen to their stories and ask the right questions. But how do you extract a story when someone doesn't even know what story to tell you? How do you gain their perspective so that you can see, hear, and feel from their vantage point the sets of causes that led them to say, "Today's the day…"? It starts with unpacking, questioning, listening, and then plugging that information into a framework that allows you to see causality.

TIPS AND TRICKS FOR TALKING TO PEOPLE—EXTRACTING PERSPECTIVE

The key is to approach the conversation as an "empty vessel"—meaning leave yourself out of the equation. Now talk, listen, and be engaged. Over the years, I developed the following tips and tricks that help me unpack, question, and listen to people's stories:

1. **Context:** When the answer feels irrational, it's typically because you don't know the whole story; the irrational becomes rational with context. "Hold on. I am confused," I'll say. You want to dig deep and get meaningful answers that explain the context that the person was in.

2. **Contrast:** Providing a person with contrast leads to greater understanding. I use a bracketing technique: "Why did you switch employers? Why not just find another role within the organization?" People will say they want easy, but they don't know how to articulate it. Ultimately, it's easier for them to tell you what's hard about something, which gives you the boundaries of easy.

3. **Unpacking:** Everything is bound. You are trying to figure out the person's reference point. One person's definition of the word "fast" may be entirely different than another's. There's no fast, only faster than… There's no healthy, only healthier than…

4. **Energy:** It's not just what people say, but how they say it. Do they accentuate words? Does the intonation go up or down? Listen for pauses and sighs. Did you hear all caps, but there are no caps? As soon as you hear this emotional energy, stop and ask further questions: "Wait, tell me more about that. Why is that important?"

5. **Use analogies:** Sometimes people will hit a wall and not have the language to express their thoughts completely. Don't push. Instead, use analogies to help build language: "How is getting a new boss like starting over?"

Ultimately, the key to any good conversation is to throw away the list of questions and to go into the conversation to discover. The best question will always come from the last answer.

TOOLS FOR UNDERSTANDING CONVERSATIONS

One of the methods that I use to unpack conversations and see causality is to evaluate the forces of progress. The forces at play determine whether people can move from A to B and make progress or not. Will it be business as usual or a new path forward? Within the forces are things that *pull* people toward change and frictions that *push* them back to the old. When we talk about people's decisions, we've found there are ultimately four forces influencing their progress.

1. **The push of the situation.** Think about the struggling moment for someone looking for a new job. What forces are pushing them toward leaving their current role?

2. **The magnetism of the new solution.** The moment they realize there might be something better—a new job that could help them make progress—that solution creates a magnetism, and they start to imagine a better life—the pull toward progress.

3. **The anxiety of the new solution.** Despite the struggle at the current job and the pull the new solution creates, there's anxiety about the unknowns of a new role. These anxieties are important because they hold people back from making progress.

4. **The habit of the present.** There are things about the current job that the person may like. This comfort and habit will hold the person back from switching.

Ultimately, you are using the forces of progress to help you unpack conversations to the point where you can answer the following: What progress are they trying to make? What is their motivation? Where is there apprehension?

Any time I talk to people about a purchase or switch that they made, I'm constantly probing for the forces of progress. The push of the situation and the magnetism of the new solution need to be stronger than their anxieties and habits before people will make a move.

SEEING AROUND CORNERS AND SEEING THROUGH SPACE AND TIME

Once you unpack, question, and listen to enough people's stories, you begin to get an omniscient, God-like perspective that allows you to see the whole. It's almost as if you are above the situation, seeing how it will play out. By understanding how people in the past made progress, you are now able to see the dominoes in the present that will cause people to behave a certain way. It's not just about having the conversations; it's about extracting the right pieces of information from those conversations—seeing the dominoes.

Overall, I conducted interviews to understand the causality behind why people change jobs. I identified hundreds of individual pushes and pulls. Then I took those forces and organized them by intent into twenty-eight core underlying causal mechanisms, (fourteen pushes and sixteen pulls):

Pushes of the current situation: why leave your current position?	Pulls of the new: what are you hoping for?
When I don't respect or trust the people I work with.	So I can have more time to spend with others in order to carry my weight.
When I feel that the work has little or no impact on the company, the world, or my life.	So my values and beliefs are aligned with the company and the people I work with.

When the way I'm managed day to day is wearing me down.	So my job fits into my existing personal life.
When my current company is struggling, and I feel the end is near.	So I can reset my life and start over.
When I end up with a new manager, and I feel like I'm starting over.	So I can get the skills for a future job/career (stepping stone).
When I feel disrespected and not trusted.	So I can be acknowledged, respected, and trusted to do great work.
When I realize I'm at a personal life event or milestone, i.e., I just turned thirty, had a child, etc.	So I can find an employer who values my experience and credentials.
When I reach a milestone at my job or career, i.e., I received my MBA, celebrated ten years at the company.	So I feel like my job is a step forward for me in the perception of others.
When my work is dominating my life and I'm sacrificing myself and my family to get things done.	So I have the freedom and flexibility to do my best work.
When a trusted advisor/mentor guides me to my next step.	So I can be recognized for my work's impact on people and the business.
When I am challenged beyond my abilities, logic, or ethics.	So I have a supportive boss who guides and provides me constructive feedback.

When I feel like I'm not challenged, or I'm bored in my current work.	So I can be part of a tight-knit team or community that I can count on.
When I can't see a place for me to go or grow in my current organization, or it will be too long/too hard.	So I can be challenged, grow, and learn on the job.
When I feel I'm on my own, ignored, and not supported.	So I am in a job that I know I can do and feel like I'm not at risk.
	So I can support my growing responsibilities.
	So I can have the time for me.

After unpacking the interviews, I realized that if any five of these pushes happened, people were likely to look for a new job. Now I have the empathetic perspective to be able to *see around corners* and *see through space and time*. (More to come on this topic in a forthcoming book on managing your career.)

What do you do with this information? For me, it's helped build a system to think about how I work with others. Now one of the ways that I structure my relationships with people who work for me is that it's all about progress—no more formal reviews. We talk about the progress that they want to make and the progress that I want to make, as well as reflect on the past progress for both. Since doing this, I find that I understand the little subtle things that help others feel progress that I did not recognize before. For example, I get pulled in a lot of different directions, and there would be points in time where I'd leave one of my employees alone with clients. Honestly, I felt badly about doing that; I thought that I might be putting her on the spot. But in reality, from her perspective, she loved those opportunities where she got to fly without a net because she knew she was ready to lead. Those moments that I'd felt guilty about actually helped her make progress more than anything else.

I use the analogy of balls and wickets in a game of croquet to help me visualize people as they move through space and time. The balls represent the people, and the wickets are the events in their life. There are spaces and times in people's lives that will cause them to need to make progress in specific ways. Because I see what they see, hear what they hear, and understand what they mean, I can now predict how future events will impact their decisions…even before they can see it. I can predict when they're going to hit a new wicket: birth of a child, advanced degree, etc. I understand the future dominoes that need to fall based on what people tell me today: "This is where you're headed…" I can say with some certainty.

MANAGING YOUR COMPANY INTERNALLY WITH EMPATHETIC PERSPECTIVE

In order for innovators and entrepreneurs to *see around corners* and *see through space and time*, they must also have supply-side empathetic perspective; demand-side alone is not enough. This starts with identifying the key players. Ask yourself: Who's involved? Why are they involved? What do they do? Internally, there are likely a multitude of roles, everything from marketing and finance to manufacturing and production surrounding your thing. Then there are external influencers such as suppliers and partners. Each of these people occupy roles on different sides of the equation, and as a result, see differently. Innovators and entrepreneurs skilled at empathetic perspective can see the whole.

HOW DO YOU SEE THE WHOLE?

My education in supply-side empathetic perspective began while struggling to find an answer to the rearview mirror problem from the Introduction. My mentor Dr. Willie Moore said, "I want you to become the molecule that becomes the plastic that then becomes the mirror." Remember the *Schoolhouse Rock!* episode "I'm Just a Bill"? It's like that.

On the surface, it may seem like an unusual exercise, but it's an incredibly brilliant way to gain supply-side empathetic perspective. Instead of asking, "What's the problem? What's the solution?" I took a step back, and I became the molecule and uncovered its journey. In doing so, I answered the critical who, what, when, where, and why, which were the first steps toward seeing the whole...

I'm the molecule. I'm made at Dow Chemicals, where they formulate me into pellets and then ship me to various plants via train. Once I arrive, I sit in the plant hopper and wait my turn. It may take days, weeks, or months, but suddenly, I get poured into a buffer that starts to heat me up. There are different pressures and temperatures as I make my way through the machine, melding together. Then I'm placed into a mold where I sit and dry for twenty seconds. Then I get popped out, cooled for a minute before getting shaped, and placed into a box. That box goes to the assembly line at the plant where I'm then placed into a car, shipped to dealers, and bought by customers.

Becoming your creation will help answer key questions: Who's involved? Why are they involved? What do they do? And not just from the perspective of the people, but also from the thing itself. It forces you to see the broader picture, which allows you to frame what's going on and understand what to do. Seeing this complexity quickly moves you from one problem/one solution to many problems and many solutions. It creates a humbleness; you realize that you don't have the answer, which stops you from assuming a solution and chasing after one hypothesis.

Oftentimes, when people go to design a product, they think there's an objectively "best" way to do it because they lack empathetic perspective on the supply-side. They don't understand the context or perspective that's wrapped around their product or service, so they're trying to find the absolute best way in which to build it. But there's no such thing as a "best" way. You must make tradeoffs. Empathetic perspective enables you to see around corners, project into the future, and therefore see the necessary tradeoffs. Without empathetic perspective, these tradeoffs become impossible.

When I sit down to help a business make progress, I say, "Tell me about your business." Invariably, they tell me about the product or service that they sell. But they need to be thinking in terms of flow: the flow of information; the flow of money, the flow of finished goods. When you understand the flow, it becomes objectively easy to see the various perspectives involved.

HOW DO YOU TEACH OTHERS TO SEE THE WHOLE?

It's not just the leader who needs empathetic perspective; your people need it as well.

Remember the red line/green line comparison in Chapter 1 for developing new cars? The manufacturer on the red line worked in individual silos. The engine designer made the best engine, and the transmission designer built the optimal transmission. They assumed that there was common understanding and agreement. The people on the red line lacked empathetic perspective, and as they got closer to launch, this played out in a very costly way.

As an innovator or entrepreneur, your people's blind spots can cost you years in development and millions in lost revenue. They need to talk to each other in deep, meaningful ways, early and often. Most organizations don't take the time to do this, and therefore, they lose site of the bigger picture. They follow a process almost blindly.

The first step is to have everyone within your organization

rotate: marketing needs to understand engineering; engineering needs to understand the assembly line, etc. Most people do not take the time to genuinely see things from other people's perspectives. It's not enough to simply talk to each other either. People need time to genuinely put themselves in each other's shoes.

Young Bob, as a fairly green engineer, thought that he had empathetic perspective. I would walk around the plant, see the assembly-line workers, talk to the engine designers, and so on, but I wasn't truly putting myself in their shoes. I'd listen, but I'd use that information to try to convince them of *my* perspective. I wanted to show them that they were wrong: "If we just did this my way, then that would work."

That's not empathetic perspective; it's a direct assault type of view.

A person with empathetic perspective doesn't initiate conversation and then go head-to-head trying to convince other people to change their mind. This is about seeing things from many perspectives, seeing the conflicts, designing new ways to work, and creating a win-win for both. People with empathetic perspective try to see where other people are coming from to understand what is going to happen. And they recognize that *they* might be the one who is wrong.

There's a lot of humbleness and curiosity embedded in empathetic perspective.

SEEING THE WHOLE: INTERNALLY AND EXTERNALLY

Innovators and entrepreneurs skilled at empathetic perspective can see the whole internally and externally. Recently, I talked to a friend who did an early test read of this book who underscored this point.

As the head of digital at a major corporation, he'd come to a stalemate with a group of engineers on a particular project. Basically, he kept insisting on changes, and they kept insisting that they were impossible. After reading this chapter, he realized that while he was very sensitive to the customer's perspective, he was less so toward the engineers.

At the next meeting, he decided to walk in with his empathetic perspective hat on. He listened to their anxieties and asked probing questions. In the end, they talked about everything but the database that was in question. After understanding their fears, together they scoped the project in a very different way, effectively ending the stalemate.

"Look, in the past, I always put my agenda first and let them react instead of understanding their perspective, but now that's all changed, and our meetings are more productive," he told me. "I realize that I need to understand the progress that they are trying to make first."

That's the real value in empathetic perspective. It shows you how to build alignment, and it shows you where there are gaps in the alignment so that you can work on those spaces. But if you don't dig deeply and apply rigor, you will miss the real meaning behind what people are trying to say; people will say one thing when they mean another. Without the proper rigor, you will inadvertently apply your own perspective to other people's words.

People skilled at empathetic perspective not only listen and question, but they also employ tools that help them unpack the causality, which ultimately allows them to *see around corners and see through space and time.*

While all five of the skills have immense value, in my experience, without empathetic perspective, you will struggle to be successful in any of the other four skills as they all build off empathetic perspective. Not a day goes by that I do not use empathetic perspective.

MAKING IT REAL

Let's summarize the chapter by comparing young Bob with enlightened Bob—contrast to create meaning. Think of it as a scale from one to ten, with young Bob at a one and enlightened Bob at a ten. Most people are somewhere in between. Where are you?

1. EMPATHETIC PERSPECTIVE

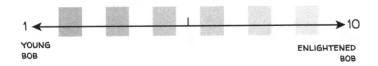

1 ⟵ ——————————————— ⟶ 10

**YOUNG
BOB**   **ENLIGHTENED
BOB**

Young Bob viewed empathetic perspective as listening and understanding in order to convince others that my way was the right way; I listened to learn how to handle their objections; I did not seek to understand; I sought to be understood.

Whereas enlightened Bob views empathetic perspective more like an actor. I want to detach from my own thought process and ask the right questions so that I understand the context that makes the irrational behavior rational. I'm trying to connect the dots so that I can see the tradeoffs and understand the future problems that I might have. I'm not trying to convince anyone to do anything.

Now, let's look at some ways that you can advance your ability to see empathetically; I recommend practicing the conversation techniques taught above. Remember, your goal is to be an empty vessel: talk, interact, unpack, and see what they are trying to do.

- Pick a family member and try to understand their perspective on any topic.

  ○ Talk to your child and uncover the progress that they want to make with school or a sport. What are their goals? It's been a long time since you were a kid, and the reality of their perspective is completely different than what you experienced.

  ○ Talk to a grandparent to uncover a big moment in their life. Try to empathetically understand why that moment was important.

○   The next time that you have a disagreement, pull out this
    tool and make sure that you understand the situation
    from the other person's perspective without judgment or
    attempting to change their mind.

•   Now, go to a place where you are unfamiliar, maybe a vaca-
    tion in a city or country very dissimilar to where you live,
    and interact with people. Immersing yourself in different
    scenarios enables you to see empathetically.

Aside from conversing with people, you can also consider taking
an improv class; playing different roles and being in different con-
texts helps immensely. Also, you can read a story from a different
time and place, like *The Adventures of Huckleberry Finn*, and try to
understand the main character's motivations and emotions.

Here are some resources to help continue your education into
empathetic perspective:

•   *Six Thinking Hats* by Edward de Bono

•   *The Design of Everyday Things* by Don Norman

•   *Creativity: Flow and the Psychology of Discovery and Invention*
    by Mihaly Csikszentmihalyi

•   *Emotional Intelligence: Why It Can Matter More Than IQ* by
    Daniel Goleman

•   *Never Split the Difference: Negotiating As If Your Life
    Depended On It* by Chris Voss

Empathetic perspective naturally drives you into uncovering
demand. But first, let me introduce my mentor Dr. Willie Moore,
a person who taught me a great deal about empathetic perspective.

Meet
DR. WILLIE HOBBS MOORE

When I met Dr. Willie Moore at the car giant, she was a manager in supplier quality assurance and worked directly with Taguchi and Deming. She was the person who made stuff happen—and I was one of many engineers who was assigned to work with her. As an engineer and the first female African American to earn a doctorate in particle physics from the university of Michigan, Willie pushed the limits society set for her when it came to race and gender. This was the 1980s, and even today, women only represent about 20 percent of the workforce in car manufacturing. So Willie had a unique perspective on the world.

She set extremely high standards for herself and had high expectations of me as well. She would tell me, "I have to be better than everybody else because they've already prejudged me as a black woman." There are very few people who I've come across either before or after Willie who possessed such high personal standards, and as a result, she pushed me extremely hard too.

Just three weeks into my full-time employment, Willie turned to me as we headed into a management meeting and said, "I want you to take responsibility for this new problem that just came up; I want you take the blame."

"Me?" I asked in surprise.

"Trust me," she said. "I know how it's going to play out."

When management asked, "Who will take on this problem," you could hear a pin drop. Everyone lowered their head and tried not to make eye contact—no one wanted this responsibility. Terrified that this move would lead to the shortest employment history ever, I dutifully obeyed and raised my hand.

"Wait, you're taking it?" the executive said in disbelief.

When we left the room, Willie said, "Now you have all the power to solve this problem." In her view, me taking the problem had nothing but upside. "No one's going to fire a twenty-two-year-old engineer who's willing to step into the burning building," she said. "Especially when none of the tenured engineers would even fess up." In her view, if I solved it, I was the hero; if I failed, there was nothing lost. Further, the tenured engineers wanted me to succeed; they didn't want it to fall back on them, so everyone rushed in to help.

In the end, Willie was right, and her approach allowed me to fast-track. People saw me as the person who was never afraid to take on a problem. Throughout the years, Willie and I developed a great friendship.

CHAPTER THREE

UNCOVERING DEMAND

"What people in business think they know about the customer and the market is likely to be more wrong than right...the customer rarely buys what the business thinks it sells."

—**Peter Drucker**, Father of Modern Management

What's the difference between a Snickers and a Milky Way? On the surface, these two products seem similar. They're both candy bars that are made in the same plant with chocolatey ingredients and sit side by side in the candy aisle. When viewed from the supply-side, they seem to compete with one another. So why would someone buy a Snickers versus a Milky Way? As it turns out, the *who, what, when, where,* and *why*—the context in which people buy a Snickers versus a Milky Way—is completely different.

Typically, people buy a Snickers when they're hungry, missed the last meal, running out of energy, lots to do, and short on time; they need a boost. Snickers fits this situation quite well because it feels like food—the nougat, caramel, and peanuts form a ball when you chew it, and you swallow it like food. As the Snickers hits your stomach, the growling and hunger pangs stop because that ball absorbs the acid in the stomach and gives the body the energy it needs. If you go to almost any vending machine at a Silicon Valley startup, the Snickers is usually gone. Snickers competes with a cup of coffee, a Red Bull, or a sandwich.

Conversely, a Milky Way converts into almost a liquid within three chews and slides down your throat, coating your mouth with chocolate and endorphins. It can take as long as twenty minutes to eat, and you savor the experience; it's a candy bar. People usually eat it alone, after an emotional event, good or bad, and it helps them take a minute to regroup and feel better or acts as a reward. Milky Way competes with ice cream, brownies, and a glass of wine.

Snickers and Milky Way are fundamentally different in terms of the struggling moment that they solve and therefore the demand that they fulfill.

Understanding this dynamic was a game changer for Snickers. They launched a commercial that spoke to people in this struggling moment. The advertisement opened on a field with a group of young men playing football with Betty White. Betty's struggling. Everyone's yelling at her. Then someone hands a Snickers bar to her. She takes a bite and transforms back into "himself"—another one of the young men. "You're not YOU when you're hungry," the narrator says. "Snickers satisfies!"

Once Snickers uncovered the demand and began marketing to people in their struggling moment, sales skyrocketed. Snickers is now the bestselling candy bar in its category with over $4 billion in sales. I would say Snickers is not a candy bar; it's fuel.

THE DIFFERENCE BETWEEN SUPPLY AND DEMAND

To uncover demand, you must understand way more than *who* your customer is. What's *causing* them to make a purchase? It's understanding value from the customer-side of the world, as opposed to the product-side of the world. It's about realizing the progress that people are trying to make based on their context. Your product or services are merely part of their solution. Demand is *caused* by a struggling moment and the thought, "Maybe I can do better..." Without the struggling moment, there is no demand. Demand is framed by who, when, where, and why.

Supply-Side vs. Demand-Side Innovation

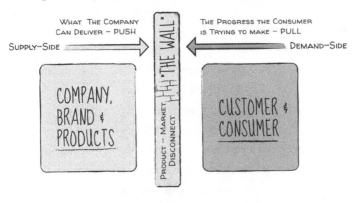

The problem arises when you are solely focused on the supply-side view of your product or service and see everything through that lens: How do I make it? How do I position it? How do I measure it? How profitable is it? In this scenario, the consumer is nebulous—an imagined, personified version of the customer—an aggregated set of demographic and psychographic information. You aggregate and triangulate the consumer around the product through *correlative* data. You think of your creation in terms of competitive sets within a category or industry. If Mars, Inc. had viewed Snickers from the supply-side, they would have focused on Milky Way as the competition and taken an entirely different approach than the Betty White commercial. They would have zeroed in on making Snickers more delicious—taste-testing Milky Way and Snickers side by side, comparing ingredients, and tweaking the contents. In the end, they would have had two candy bars that were a parody of each other, missing a $4 billion opportunity.

When you innovate from the demand side, you realize that the customer has a completely different perspective. They usually have a completely different reference point of your product (think Snickers versus Red Bull instead of Snickers versus Milky Way). Their context revolves around the new desired outcomes they seek, and their competitive sets aren't actually competitive sets but candidate sets: "I can do this, or I can do that." The customer has no idea how Snickers bars are made, and they don't care. In most cases, they can't tell you that a Snickers would even solve their struggling moment until they've tried it or until you step in to let them know.

Both supply and demand are important perspectives. In fact, as an innovator or entrepreneur, you need both, but in my experience, most innovators and entrepreneurs are more focused and skilled at the supply-side. It's critical that you understand how demand works. How does your product or service fit into people's lives?

THE PROBLEM WITH SUPPLY-SIDE-ONLY THINKING

What are the consequences of taking a wholly supply-side approach?

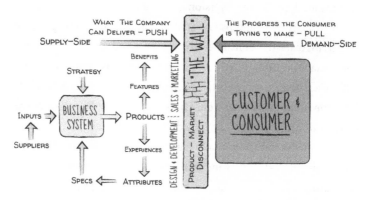

SUPPLY–SIDE VS. DEMAND–SIDE INNOVATION

Let's take a trip back in time for this example. The year is 2010, and I'm sitting on the cold, metal bleachers at my daughter's ice hockey game. She's poised to take a slap shot from the point, and I quickly snap a picture. "It's blurry again," I say to my wife Julie in utter frustration. All I want is an action shot of my daughter on the rink, but each time I try, the results are the same: crap.

That afternoon, I decide it's time to buy a new camera, a good camera, so I get online and pull up Canon's website. They have dozens of cameras to choose from, pictured side by side, showcasing each camera's image processing, megapixels, and shutter speed. Then there are software options for developing the pictures. It's confusing. I don't understand this lingo, and I have no interest in taking the time to learn it. I just want to take great pictures.

Frustrated, I turn to Nikon and Sony, only to find that their websites are virtual mirror images of Canon's. Ugh! I don't have time for this. It feels like a rabbit hole I don't want to go in.

Thankfully, along comes Apple. They make a high-quality camera, attach it to my phone so that it's always with me, and make it easy to take great pictures—point and click. They don't talk to me about image processing, megapixels, or shutter speed, and they even include the software.

Now Canon would say that they know photography the best. Yet Apple walked in the door and with one button, took their business away. In 2010, camera sales were 121 million units. By 2018, they'd sunk to 19 million units, but during the same timeframe, demand for taking pictures actually skyrocketed by almost a hundred times with social media.

Canon, Nikon, and Sony were so focused on competing—the supply-side—that they just kept adding more and more capabilities, making their products more complicated. Then they tried to force their customers to learn their language. The market rejected all three. They missed the point; people simply wanted to take great pictures. Apple, on the other hand, understood the struggling moment, saw the progress that people were trying to make, and disrupted the industry.

So, how do you uncover demand?

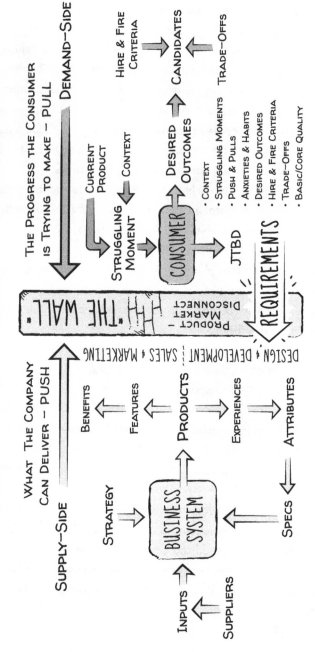

THE KEYS TO UNCOVERING DEMAND

Uncovering demand starts with interviewing customers who've used your product before and made progress. You need them to tell you the story of how they got here. What dominoes had to fall for them to say, "Today's the day..."

I uncover demand by using the Jobs to Be Done (JTBD) methodology to frame demand. The reality: there are other ways to uncover demand; JTBD is just a tool that I employ. Whether you use JTBD to uncover demand or another tool, it's the demand that's important, not the tool. You need to make that paradigm shift from your supply-side perspective to the customer's perspective. That said, a "Job" is the progress a person is trying to make in a struggling circumstance.

Recently, my friend Amrita bought a Peloton, and Greg and I sat down to understand why. Amrita is a busy, successful technology executive in her forties who lives in Toronto, Canada with her husband Bill. They own a beautiful 800-square-foot condo in an upscale building that includes a gym, but when Covid hit, Amrita found herself quarantined in her condo, and the gym closed, so she bought a $3,000 Peloton. Greg and I wanted to uncover the framework for how Amrita made the decision to buy. The following is a brief snippet of our hour-long conversation.

Bob: Can you tell us a little about your exercise background?

Amrita: My days are busy. I've struggled for a while to find enough time to exercise. I used to be a long-distance runner; I loved running; I was "addicted" to it. But now my body feels different, and it's become more uncomfortable to run.

Bob: How long is a while?

Amrita: At least four years. I kept starting and stopping; I'd start running, then stop. I'd try a class but drop it. I haven't gotten over that hump and really gotten back into shape.

Greg: Why is exercise important to you? What does exercise do for you?

Amrita: I would say out of vanity, for sure; I want to be a certain weight and size. Slowly, over the recent years, I've put on weight. Also, after I turned forty, I became more conscious of the importance of maintaining a healthy life.

Greg: You said a "healthy" life. Everyone defines healthy differently. Can you describe to me what that means to you?

Amrita: I work with a lot of people who are much younger than me. I find that if we are doing a team activity, hiking for instance, I'm conscious of the fact that I am not in as good of physical condition as they are. I also want to avoid the problems that come with aging when you are too sedentary.

Greg: Are putting on weight and keeping up with others the same or different issues?

Amrita: I think they are related. My weight impacts my comfort. When I was twenty pounds lighter, it was easier. But I would say it's the long-term health that I'm focused on and feeling good about the clothes that I'm wearing. I love clothes and fashion, and I'm not used to my body being this shape. It limits my options.

Bob: When did you buy the Peloton?

Amrita: Last week. About a month before that, I asked my husband Bill, "Do you think we should get an exercise bike?" And he said, "No." He felt like our condo was too small and pointed out that we already had a gym in the building, even though it's Covid, and the gym is closed. I dropped the idea and instead decided to buy a TRX. It's a piece of exercise equipment that you can hang on your doorframe, so it doesn't take up much space, and it's good for strength training.

Bob: When the TRX came, were you excited?

Amrita: Yes, I thought it would be a great way to get exercise without leaving my condo. I was new to the TRX, so I googled a few exercises.

Greg: Before Covid, what kind of exercises did you do at the gym?

Amrita: I would usually run a little on the treadmill and then walk or do some strength training with weights.

Greg: So the TRX gave you the strength training, but it didn't give you the cardio?

Amrita: Exactly. I missed the treadmill as a way to have my "me" time and just be with my own thoughts. The TRX was helpful, but it wasn't enough.

Bob: So why not get a treadmill if you know that you like that?

Amrita: Right, I don't normally even go on an exercise bike, but my husband does. I thought that if I got a bike, he would be more likely to use it too. And I didn't think a treadmill would even fit in our condo. There's no place to put something that big. Plus, for a while now, running has not been working for me. I wanted to find something that I could get addicted to again like the running.

Bob: So what happened in the days leading up to the purchase that brought you back to the Peloton?

Amrita: For weeks, I had seen friends on social media post about their Pelotons and how addicted they were to them. Then the day before I bought it, I was scrolling Instagram and my friend who is similar in age and fitness level posted about her Peloton: "I love being able to get a quick twenty-minute workout between meetings." As soon as I saw it, I knew that I wanted to buy one.

Bob: So what happened next?

Amrita: I was concerned that there wasn't space for the Peloton. But I have this trunk sitting in my office that was a gift from my father-in-law. I realized that if we moved the trunk to Bill's office, I could put the Peloton there.

Bob: How did Bill get swung from a no to a yes?

Amrita: We were sitting watching TV, and I pointed out that we hadn't been getting our exercise for a while now and that I thought a bike would be a good idea. Plus, we were saving $2,000 from a vacation that needed to be canceled due to Covid. I suggested moving the trunk, and he said okay, so I bought it.

People might say what happened here is just the perfect storm, but it's very predictable. Let's unpack this interview into the three key frameworks for how people buy.

1. The three sources of energy or motivations (functional, emotional, and social)

2. The four forces of progress (push, pull, anxiety, and habit forces)

3. The Job To Be Done timeline (sequence of events and actions to make progress)

THE THREE SOURCES OF ENERGY OR MOTIVATIONS

There are three different categories of motivation: functional, emotional, and social. Let's discuss how each of the three play out in Amrita's buying process. Think of it as the energy or fuel to make the buying process happen.

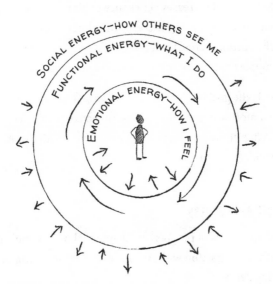

1. **Functional Motivation:** How cumbersome is the purchasing process for the buyer—time, effort, and speed? I think of mechanical things here: speed, effort, steps, etc. Peloton made the purchase easy. Although I didn't include this portion of the interview, Amrita told us that she had one conversation with Peloton before making the purchase, and setting up the bike was included in the delivery. Amrita just needed to find a place for the bike in her home—move that trunk.

2. **Emotional Motivation:** What positive, or negative, internal thoughts are driving my purchase—fears, frustrations, and desires? For Amrita, this purchase was driven by her emotional motivations more than anything else. She had insecurity about her weight and physical ability to keep up. Amrita missed her alone time that the treadmill provided, and she also longed for that feeling of being addicted to exercise, like running.

3. **Social Motivations:** How do other people perceive, respect, trust, or acknowledge me? Amrita chooses a bike in great part to get Bill from a "no" to a "yes." She knows that he likes to bike, so it increases her chance of his buy-in. Amrita also talked about the live classes with Peloton (not included in the portion shared) and how she longed for that community support to help her get back into regular exercise.

Overall, the goal is to reduce the negative functional, emotional, and social motivations, which are causing anxiety and serving as a barrier. While at the same time, amplifying the positive motivations to create pull for the product or service.

THE FORCES OF PROGRESS

I detailed the forces of progress in Chapter 2, but let's apply it once again to the conversation with Amrita as it's a critical component to uncovering demand.

Causation – JTBD Forces of Progress

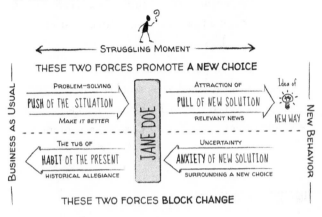

1. **The push of the situation.** Think about the struggling moment for Amrita. What forces were pushing her toward buying a Peloton? The gym closed, and Amrita was facing a long period of time without access to exercise equipment. Lately, she'd been feeling older, not able to keep up physically, or fit into clothes like she used to. Additionally, Amrita was no longer able to run as exercise.

2. **The magnetism of the new solution.** The moment she realized that something might get her back to a fitter lifestyle and help her make progress, the solution created magnetism; she started to imagine a better life where she felt and looked more like her younger self. She started noticing her friends rave on social media about being "addicted" and getting in a quick twenty-minute workout between meetings. This spoke to Amrita—the pull toward progress.

3. **The anxiety of the new solution.** Despite her struggle and the pull the new solution created, there was anxiety. Could she get Bill to agree to the bike? How could she justify

the cost? Where was she going to put the Peloton in an 800-square-foot apartment? These anxieties are important because they hold people back from making the progress that they need.

4. **The habit of the present.** Her current gym was closed, but eventually it would open. Would she decide later that she wanted to go back to the gym and regret the Peloton? Would she love biking as much as she loved running?

THE TIMELINE FOR PROGRESS

The forces and the motivations drive decisions, but not in a vacuum. Ultimately, you need to see the way that people buy as a system that plays out over time. People must be in the right time and place in their life. Nothing is random! Through the years, I've uncovered the six stages a buyer must walk through before making a purchase:

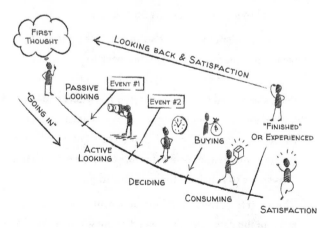

JTBD TIMELINE – THE PROCESS OF MAKING PROGRESS

1. First Thought—creating the space in the brain

2. Passive Looking—learning

3. Active Looking—seeing the possibilities

4. Deciding—making the tradeoffs and establishing value

5. Onboarding—the act of doing the JTBD, meeting expectations, and delivering satisfaction and value

6. Ongoing Use—building the habit

Imagine the events that Amrita detailed in her interview like huge dominoes falling. What made her say "Today's the day…"? You need to understand *causality*. What are the events that pushed and pulled her to move forward or backward?

First Thought

When you finally have that first thought: "I'm not fitting into my clothes," or "I can't keep up with others physically." Whether you say it out loud, or you have it in your head, it's the critical first step for people to buy. Before this first step, there's not a place in your mind to file the information about treadmills or bikes.

Amrita realized for a long time that she needed to take action and exercise, but it wasn't until she could no longer go to the gym and didn't have an outlet that she thought of owning exercise equipment. She briefly imagined a bike, but when Bill vetoed the idea, she quickly moved on to the TRX. Amrita's actual first thought about a bike happened when the TRX arrived and did not provide her the cardio outlet.

Once you have the first thought, you've opened-up the space in your mind for the information. Without this first thought, there is no demand. But once you have it, you notice things you didn't notice before, which causes you to transition to passive looking.

Passive Looking

> "Questions are places in your mind where answers fit. If you haven't asked the question, the answer has nowhere to go. It hits your mind and bounces right off. You have to ask the question—you have to want to know—in order to open up the space for the answer to fit."
>
> **—Dr. Clayton Christensen**

The first thought is how you create the space. Passive looking is how you start to fill the space. Because Amrita had the first thought, she noticed her friends' Instagram posts about the Peloton. She remembered feeling addicted to running and saw that same energy in their posts. Then Amrita's friend posted, "I love being able to get a quick twenty-minute workout between meetings." The clincher!

People can passively look for years if there's no event pushing them to the next step on the timeline. Whatever the event, it acts like a domino falling in your life that moves you along the timeline to active looking. Now Amrita was in active looking.

Active Looking

Active looking is when people plan, spend time, and even spend money figuring out what's next—the solution to their struggling moment. Here's where Amrita went on the Peloton website to try and figure out cost, delivery, and setup. At this stage, Amrita is understanding the discrete, independent features and attributes of the Peloton and starts connecting the dots to frame future tradeoffs.

Deciding

This is where people make their tradeoffs and ultimately decide what they want. When buying, there's no ideal solution, every customer makes tradeoffs. Part of the journey is understanding the tradeoffs people are willing to make.

Amrita needs to figure out how to fit the Peloton into her 800-square-foot apartment. She decides that she can fit the Peloton in her office if she finds a place for the trunk, which was a gift from her father-in-law. Amrita also needs to rationalize the $3,000 cost. The fact that she needs to cancel a $2,000 vacation fits this narrative perfectly.

Onboarding

Onboarding is where the rubber hits the road. It's where the consumer determines if you've met the expectations set when they decided to lock in and buy your product or service. Whatever expectations were set are now poured in concrete. In onboarding, the consumer is having their first use of the product or service and measuring that against their expectations to see if they bought what they think they bought. When I interviewed Amrita, the Peloton had not arrived yet, but she will likely compare it to the TRX and judge if she is getting a good cardio workout. She will also critique those first live classes and measure whether or not they provide the community support she craved.

Ongoing Use

There's a difference between buying and onboarding a product or service and using a product or service every day—ongoing use. How well did you satisfy expectations? The satisfaction is determined by the expectations set. If Peloton did not set expectations well, Amrita will have new struggling moments. Ongoing use is where the jobs get done and the progress is achieved. Does Amrita get addicted to the Peloton? Does she fit into her clothes better over time? Can she keep up on a hike? These are likely the metrics Amrita will use to measure progress.

WHAT'S YOUR CUSTOMER'S VALUE CODE?

Oftentimes innovators talk to people but do so through the lens of their product and its features and benefits: Why is this feature important? What does it help you do? And then they think they understand the buyer. You hear things like, it's easy to use, I love the interface, etc. They go deeper and deeper into the product with you. That's not uncovering demand.

Uncovering demand is about you going into their lives. It's about uncovering their struggling moment, the outcome they seek, and the progress that they are trying to make. Does it help them? It's about the who, what, when, where, and why of how your product helps them, the job they are hiring your product to do.

If I asked, "Do you like steak, or do you like pizza?" You might say, "I like both," right? So let's talk about a steak situation versus a pizza situation. Typically, you're having a steak when it's been a rough week and you want to reward yourself, or you're celebrating a special occasion. You're going to cook it a special way and maybe have guests; it's an event. A pizza situation looks entirely different: I've got four kids; I need to feed them, drive to soccer, and get home-work done. If you try to stick steak into that scenario, it's horrible, and vice versa.

What you realize is that you like both steak and pizza, but if you take the pizza and put it in the steak situation, the value changes. Value is a function of the context, outcome, progress, and effort. Uncovering demand is seeing value from the customer's perspective as opposed to value from the product perspective. And it's not about what people value. It's about who, what, when, where, and why people value.

Once you can see value from the customer's perspective, you realize that value is not a feature or a benefit. It's a tradeoff people make depending on the context they are in. You can't understand tradeoffs unless you know your customer's value code. Once you understand that people value pizza in certain situations, you can see that they will not pay a lot more for better pizza. But steak, now that's a different story.

As an innovator or entrepreneur, you need to understand how your product or service fits into people's lives—demand. But you still need to understand the supply-side: How do I make it? How do I position it? How do I measure it? How profitable is it? The what, how, and how much of product. Innovators and entrepreneurs need to understand both sides, but I've found the supply-side tends to come easily—it's almost a given. Successful innovators and entrepreneurs understand how to separate the demand-side from the supply-side. As a result, they can see and manage the necessary tradeoffs.

MAKING IT REAL

Let's summarize again by comparing young Bob with enlightened Bob.

2. UNCOVERING DEMAND

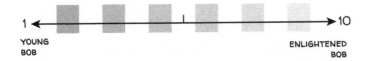

1 ←————————————|—————————→ 10
YOUNG
BOB
ENLIGHTENED
BOB

Young Bob believed that supply created demand, and therefore, I thought that my responsibility was to convince people to buy my product. I was more worried about personas, correlation, and size of market than actually understanding the progress that people were trying to make. I wanted to scale quickly: how can I make this as big as possible, as fast as possible?

Enlightened Bob, however, wants to understand how to add value one person at a time. Only then, when I can see the hidden patterns, can I think about scale. I know that my product does not create demand; demand is created by a struggling moment where people have a space to fill; I create value by understanding how to fill that space.

Where are you on the journey to uncovering demand? Maybe you've nailed it. Maybe you still need some help. Ask yourself these clarifying questions:

- Do I understand how my product or service fits into people's lives?

- Do I understand how my customer's context can add value?

- Am I defining value as the progress that people are trying to make?

- What are the tradeoffs my customers are willing to make for that progress?

Here are some resources to help continue your education into uncovering demand:

- *Demand-Side Sales 101: Stop Selling and Help Your Customers Make Progress* by Bob Moesta with Greg Engle

- *Competing Against Luck: The Story of Innovation and Customer Choice* by Clayton Christensen

- *Talking to Humans: Success starts with understanding your customers* by Giff Constable

- *The End of Average: How We Succeed in a World That Values Sameness* by Todd Rose

- *The Human Element: Overcoming the Resistance That Awaits New Ideas* by David Schonthal and Loran Nordgren

Once we understand demand, it's a question of how we go about servicing that demand: What do we build? That leads us naturally into our next chapter, causal structures.

But first, let me introduce my mentor Dr. Clayton Christensen, a master at uncovering demand.

Meet
DR. CLAYTON CHRISTENSEN

Of my four mentors, I met Dr. Clayton Christensen last. I had left the car giant and branched out on my own to build new products, but there was a vacuum in the place that Taguchi, Deming, and Moore had once held. That's precisely when I was introduced to Clay, who was in his first-year teaching at the Harvard Business School. Clay had just gotten his PhD at forty-two, a father of five.

Clay was a giant of a man, standing at six feet, eight inches tall, but as kind as they come; he matched the definition of a gentle giant. The first time I shook his hand, mine just disappeared—that's how big he was. Clay loved to talk to people who were not afraid to ask him questions, so in that respect, we were a perfect match; I'm endlessly curious. At our first meeting, we sat down and talked at length about our combined passion for building products that could help people. But we came at it from different vantage points: Clay was an academic, passionate about building better management theory, whereas I was an engineer—a practitioner—I'd rather go learn by building.

In the beginning, I saw Clay as an advisor, teacher, and mentor. Once every quarter, I'd take the trip from Detroit to Boston and spend four uninterrupted hours learning from him. Over time—our relationship spanned twenty-seven years—I considered him to be one of my best friends and a brother.

Clay taught me about disruptive innovation, which I will detail in the next chapter, and we helped each other make progress. Every time I saw him, he'd ask, "What can I do to help you?" He wanted to delve into my struggling moments, and I wanted to do the same for him. I became his ear to the ground by finding him businesses and people to talk to that helped advance his research in management theory.

Together, Clay and I—with the help of others like Karen Dillon, David Duncan, and Taddy Hall—architected the "Jobs to Be Done" (JTBD) theory, which is a framework that helps you understand why and how people buy the products they do. He was the theory builder, and I was the practitioner. He then brought the theory to life for the world when he published *Competing Against Luck*. It turned concepts that I sometimes still struggle to explain into something people can understand and adopt.

Clay taught me how to take the foundation from Taguchi, Deming, and Moore and think about it more broadly—apply theory to it. I'm an engineer; I just build things. Until that point, I didn't quite grasp the notion of theory. I could connect dots between my problem-solving and see the similarities, but I didn't recognize it as a theory. Clay was all about building new management theory. That's what he set out to do in this world.

CHAPTER FOUR

CAUSAL STRUCTURES

"If you can't describe what you are doing as a process, you don't know what you're doing."

—**Dr. W. Edwards Deming**

"Do you know the difference between correlation and causation?" Taguchi asked me one morning as we shared breakfast while traveling for work. These were still the days of "young Bob," and I relished the opportunity to pick his brain.

CORRELATION ≠ CAUSATION

"I use correlation to find causation; they're the same thing?" I responded.

"No. They're very different, and if you confuse them, you may end up doing more harm than good." Then he proceeded to tell me an old Japanese story about the...wind.

Apparently, hundreds of years ago, Japanese cultures believed that trees *caused* the wind. Because they needed the wind for fishing, they prohibited people from cutting down any trees for any reason. It was not until they understood that it was, in fact, the wind that caused the trees to move that they could move forward and make progress. That's correlation versus causation. The wind and the trees moving together is correlative, but which comes first—the *cause*—is way more important.

Causal structures are rooted in the notion of cause and effect.

THE IMPORTANCE OF CAUSE AND EFFECT

There's a mystic quality to seeing cause and effect, especially for innovators and entrepreneurs. People will say, "You're a fortune teller." The truth is, I have no magic; I don't have telepathy. But I do have a framework for seeing causal structures, which allows me to put the bright pieces together and say, "When this and that happen, here's the effect…"

For many years, for instance, I have studied how people and companies respond to major events where they have no idea what's going to happen next: Gulf War, 9/11, etc. Then Covid hit, and the country locked down. Because I understood cause and effect in similar scenarios, it became easy to predict responses even before the events unfolded. I didn't know the timing—the when—but I could frame the phases of how the world would respond, identify the triggers to move to the next phase, and then adjust my business accordingly.

I knew that businesses would first, undoubtedly, hunker down: "This is going to be over in three months," they'd think as they sat and waited for someone else to react. But they'd miss the details behind the scenes: What would happen when the lockdown ended? People certainly would not go back to business as usual because they would be afraid. That anxiety and apprehension would drive their decisions. For instance, it was predictable that when restaurants reopened, people would suddenly be concerned about crowds. Whether or not state governments restricted capacity and to what extent, restaurants needed to operate at 50 percent capacity for their own good. If they didn't, people would go home, but most businesses waited for instruction and watched their competition. They could not see the causal structures.

Similarly, during lockdown, people had to work from home. As a result, companies had to put systems in place to make remote work possible. Before this, many companies feared their people could not be trusted to work from home. Then businesses kept moving despite remote work. Suddenly, it was clear that people could be trusted. Now, when the crisis dissipates, there will be a new normal; it might be helpful to gather as a company sometimes, but the notion that it must be five days a week will change.

Causal mechanisms also predict the rise and fall of certain businesses during Covid. The adoption of virtual meetings taught everyone how to share their screen. Gone are the days of printing materials and handing them out. Will printers become obsolete? Likely. Meanwhile, sales for green screens, computers, video cameras, etc. have gone up. People are working from home; they need to look professional. Green screens allow them to take their remote conferences to the next level by putting up digital images behind them. But few companies will focus on the cause of the change, and rather just the effect: people are buying green screens. They will continue to speak to their customers about the features and benefits of their green screen over the competition as opposed to meeting them in their struggling moment: Why do people need a green screen? What are the causal structures that led them to buy a green screen in the first place? Not Covid, but...

Innovators and entrepreneurs skilled at causal structures understand the cause and the effect as well as the sequence of events that need to happen. If I were to build an icon for causal structures, it would be dominoes falling. What are the dominoes that have to fall before people say, "Today's the day…" Innovators and entrepreneurs skilled at causal structures don't panic in uncertain times because they can see what others can't, and can therefore reasonably predict how events will unfold. They may not know exactly when things will happen, but they understand how. They're not anxious; they're confident and able to make better decisions as a result.

Causal structures are so embedded in my thought process that I apply them to everything in my life. Maybe you already do this as well.

Think about the last time you and your spouse got dressed up for an event. "Wow, you look amazing," you say enthusiastically. But despite your praise, their response is mild, "Thanks," they say, largely unmoved. At first, you think nothing of this interaction, but then you arrive at your event and a friend pays them a remarkably similar compliment. "You look stunning!" This time, however, your spouse is overjoyed.

Now on one level, this could bother you, right? But not if you understand the underlying causal structure. When you get familiar with people, they discount your responses because they know what you're going to say. I call it the spousal discount. It's the same reason we have outside consultants in business. I can go into a company and say the same thing somebody on the inside has been saying forever, but when I say it, people respond like it's new and novel: "That's amazing!" It has nothing to do with me and everything to do with the relationship. Once you recognize a causal structure, you can use it to your advantage to help people make progress.

Innovators and entrepreneurs skilled at causal structures observe the cause-and-effect phenomenon and utilize it to help them make progress, but to see causal structures you need to be able to take a step back and see the whole as a system.

UNPACKING CAUSE AND EFFECT WITH SYSTEMS THINKING

"Each system is perfectly designed to give you exactly what you are getting today."

—Dr. W. Edwards Deming

Causal structures are a fundamental view of how something works, which is ultimately about systems thinking. So what is a system?

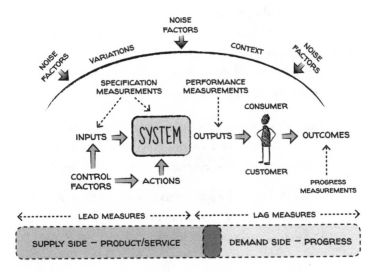

Look at the diagram above and imagine the "system" as a black box where all the action takes place.

- There are inputs to the black box.

- There are outputs from the black box.

- And there are outcomes for the person buying your product or service.

Think of a car's braking system, for example. When you want the car to stop, you press the brake. That's the input to the system. When the car slows down—deceleration—that's the output from the system. The outcome is to slow the car to make a turn. In between the input and output resides the system where all the action takes place—the black box: The pedal must be stiff enough to displace the plunger. The plunger must put pressure on a piston, the fluid pressure goes up, and the calipers push the brake pads against the rotors, creating heat and friction, thus slowing the car down.

Innovators and entrepreneurs skilled at causal structures take a step back and see the whole. Not only do they understand the inputs (resources), outputs (products), as well as the outcomes (results), but they also understand their sphere of influence—control factors and noise factors. Here's a recap from the Introduction:

- Control factors are parameters of a system you can change that impact the system's performance, and you have the ability, responsibility, and control to set them—specifications.

- Noise factors are the parameters that impact the system that you cannot control, choose not to control, or are too expensive to control—operating limits.

Let's look back at the rearview mirror example. Young Bob struggled to solve the problem because I did not have a system to unpack causal structures. I focused on the problem rather than the function of the mirror. Taguchi taught me that to solve the problem, I needed to look at the system as a whole and ask myself the following:

- What are the inputs?

- What are the outputs?

- What are the outcomes?

- How do I understand my sphere of influence?

- How do I design it to work in the face of noise factors?

- What do I measure?

Now this is where I'm going to sound a bit like a math professor. The rearview mirror's system is part of a bigger system called the "super-system." Within the super-system are things like the wind-shield, interior dashboard, etc. Additionally, within the rearview mirror itself, there are "subsystems," including the lens, case, set screw, etc.

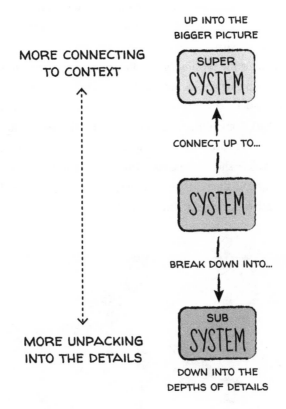

Understanding your system with inputs, outputs, noise factors, and control factors gives you a 360-degree view. Add to that an understanding of your thing within the larger context of super-systems and subsystems, and now you have a 720-degree view—an omniscient perspective.

$$\circlearrowleft 360 \circlearrowright \ + \ \circlearrowleft 360° \ = \ \circlearrowleft 720 \circlearrowright$$

When you conceptualize your thing in this manner, you can clearly see the boundaries, which naturally shows you your sphere of influence; I have these inputs, I want these outputs, and I am responsible for what's going on in between.

Remember the red line/green line story from Chapter 1? On the red line, the engineers did not see the whole system; therefore, they each designed their thing in a vacuum. When they tried to pull it all together, something would invariably break. The transmission engineer should have been thinking of the engine as noise, and the engine engineer should have been thinking about the transmission as noise. Instead, they each made their component perfect and then blamed each other when it did not work.

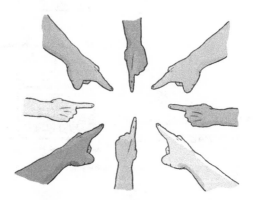

The Japanese manufacturers were able to develop their cars more quickly because they saw the entire system as a whole that was interdependent. They understood systems, super-systems, and sub-systems, and how each component connected up to each other. This enabled them to play out their innovation through time and space as well as see around corners with a 720-degree perspective.

Systems thinking is a critical tool for innovators and entrepreneurs because without it, you don't know what to work on.

Creating Through Right to Left Thinking

Most people tend to think about the system like they do time, from left to right—the way we read in the US. There's the input, the system, and the output. They think of cause and effect in the same manner: cause then effect. They then tend to design and build with that direction: what do I have, what do I need, what can I build, who needs it, and what do they value?

But the output goes to a customer who takes that output and tries to do something with it; their intended outcome. And it's that outcome that innovators and entrepreneurs should start with: "Begin with the end in mind," as Stephen Covey famously said. I call this right to left thinking.

What you really want to do when creating something new is begin from the right and move left. Let's understand the outcomes and the context by which customers are going to use the product first. This creates a set of technology-agnostic specs (what the customer wants without a solution) for the outputs that you need to create to enable the customer to make that progress. Then ask yourself, "What systems and inputs do I need to then create those outputs?" Ultimately, when you design something new, you want to move from right to left, but when you sit down to build it, everything happens left to right.

Young Bob would build the system and then test it—left to right thinking. But enlightened Bob begins with the outcomes in mind, translates them to outputs, and then takes the time to design, build, and test.

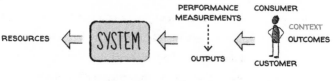

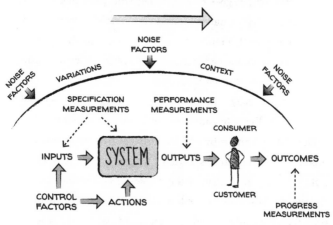

APPLYING SYSTEMS THINKING

Remember the catapult story from the Introduction? My professor wanted me to find the pull-back angle for the catapult—a simple problem to solve—but because I now understood causal structures, I wanted to make the most robust catapult that would work in the real world. So I asked myself the following:

- How does the catapult work?

- What are the inputs to the system?

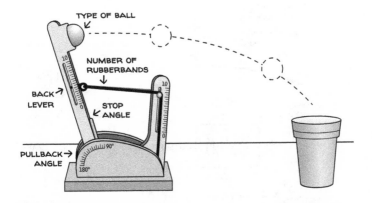

I looked at the pull-back angle of the lever. I considered one rubber band versus two and thought about stretch and wear from usage over time. What would happen if the ball size changed? What about wind resistance? Then there was the catapult height, and also cup size.

Before learning under Taguchi, young Bob would simply ask, "How far do you want it to go?" and then I'd find the distance. That's what my professor wanted. I would have tried one pull-back angle after another, testing one factor at a time—A/B testing. In the end, I would have found an answer in the laboratory setting, but my catapult wouldn't have been robust in the face of noise factors in the real world.

I see this same mentality in innovation today. Like young Bob, people test one factor at a time—A/B testing—and then wait for problems to happen, and react. They go in blind because they do not see the whole system. But when you think about the whole system, you end up testing many factors, and as a result, you end up building something that's robust. More of this to come in the next chapter— *Prototyping to Learn.*

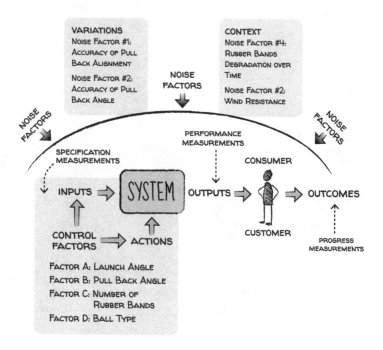

Taguchi taught me not to focus on the problem, searching for solutions like a needle in a haystack, but to focus on the function and then ask, "How do I build a catapult that is least sensitive to the things that I can't control?" Invariably, that starts with asking, "What is the outcome I want?"

The Difference Between Lead
and Lag Measures

Oftentimes we end up creating measures based on the output of our thing—lag measures—when we should be measuring the input—lead measures.

For instance, if I measure the success of the company on the profit, I'm focused solely on a lag measure, which means that I must wait and see if I got it right after the fact. Whereas if I focus on lead measures, such as sales and expenses, then profit will be almost automatic.

Think about weight loss as another example. You might weigh yourself, a lag measure to see if you're losing weight, but the reality is that if you create the right input, i.e., number of steps and calories, you can guarantee the weight loss.

When trying to build something good, you need to understand what the quality inputs are to guarantee the output.

ALTERNATIVE CAUSAL STRUCTURES

All the successful innovators and entrepreneurs that I've met along the way have two or three dominant causal structures that they use to help them unpack cause and effect.

My friend and mentor Clay Christensen had a framework for causal mechanisms called "disruptive innovation." The core questions were: What causes highly successful companies to fail and go bankrupt? How does management let this happen? What causes this to happen? How do you prevent it? Or how do you use it? It's the idea that as companies grow, they add more and more features and benefits, making their prices increase exponentially until eventually, people at the low end of the market are priced out. They want to buy their product, but they can't afford to, which leaves the company vulnerable at the low end of the market. Clay would use the story of US Steel to explain…

At one point, US Steel was by far the leader in the steel market. They manufactured a variety of different products, ranging from low-end rebar that priced at roughly $10 per pound to high-end steel that ran up to $100,000 per pound. They made all their revenue on the high end of the market. Then along came Nucor who designed an innovative method for melting old scrap metal and producing rebar at much cheaper costs. US Steel was more than happy to let the rebar business go; after all, they made no revenue off it. At the time, it seemed like a win-win.

Nucor, with their low overhead and innovative technology, started making huge returns on the rebar. And as they did, their market share continued to creep up, taking more and more of US Steel's business. During the course of about eight years, Nucor was able to eat away at 80 percent of US Steel's revenue, boxing US Steel into a high-end corner of the market until they were forced to declare bankruptcy.

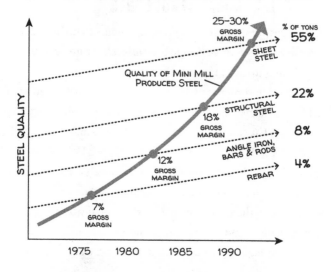

CHANGES IN MINI MILL CAPABILITIES 1970 – 2000

When companies would come to Clay as they struggled to grow their markets, he would tell them the US Steel story and ask, "Are you US Steel? Have you boxed yourself into the upper corner in a way that makes you vulnerable to disruption? Do you need to reinvent yourself and figure out how to be in the low end?"

No accountant or finance expert will tell you to build products with smaller margins, but if you understand the causal mechanisms of disruption, you realize that if you don't, your business will die.

CREATING NEW FRAMEWORKS THROUGH ANOMALIES

Most people would look at US Steel and think that's an anomaly, right? But anomalies are the way in which you build new theory and frameworks for unpacking causal structures. Anomalies show you what you don't know. This goes back to the notion of failing and learning from Chapter 1. When you fail, you create an anomaly that helps build better models for the future.

When I build something, I'm designing it using what I believe are the right causal structures. So when it does not work the way I expect it too, it's an opportunity to say, "What am I missing? What else is important that I did not see before?" Anomalies help add to your field of view.

Successful innovators and entrepreneurs, because they are grounded in cause and effect, consider and study anomalies with great interest; they recognize patterns.

THE PROBLEM WITH AN EFFECT-ONLY APPROACH

I've found that nine times out of ten, people tend to focus on the effect side of the equation, not the cause, and they do so with vague language. I'll be in a meeting, and someone will say, "We need to build trust with the customer." Trust is an outcome—an effect—and it's a vague word. So first we must define trust.

"What's trust?" I'll ask. Because if we don't define it, how can we *cause* it? So we will start to unpack trust, and people will use a lot of generic, abstract language. So I'll start to ask them to explain trust within a context: "Does trust already exist, and we're building more trust? Are we creating new trust? How do we know if someone trusts us? How do we measure trust?

It quickly becomes clear that trust by itself is a very abstract concept; you can't organize around trust. Trust depends on the context; it's subtle.

"How do you trust a salesperson?" I'll ask, to demonstrate my point.

"I don't," they'll say.

"If you don't trust salespeople, how do you buy from anybody?" I'll ask.

"I need to vet people," they'll respond.

"What do you do to vet a salesperson?" I'll ask.

As I walk through this exercise, it becomes clear that when trust exists, there are things that had to happen to enable it. Now you're in a completely different realm: to build trust, you have to do this, and to earn trust, you have to do that. Oftentimes people struggle because they are focused on the effect rather than the cause; they're not thinking deeply enough.

When I'm conducting interviews, I know that if I get people to talk about cause and effect, I can predict the future. It's the bright pieces that allow me to connect the dots. Ultimately, everything is built on cause and effect. Greg and I listen for those dominoes to fall when we interview people, the things that cause them to move from A to B and make a change. But most people miss the cause because they focus on the effect instead of the cause. When people start talking about the future, you have to understand *why* they want what they want. You have to be able to decipher the causal mechanisms behind their statements.

Everything can be seen this way. Look at the US education system. It's largely an effect-only approach.

First, there's no empathetic perspective: we *push* material onto students and test them, but we never give the context that would create the *pull* for learning. How is math applicable to their life? Why care? We recognize on one level that people have different strengths and goals but then push the same generic content onto everyone. Students struggle to make progress because they don't understand why they are learning half of what's being taught. There's no pull.

The education system is caught up in the process of teaching and not the process of learning. They believe their job is to supply knowledge as opposed to helping people learn. Why? They're not seeing the whole picture, and therefore they focus on the wrong things. They want students to learn—the effect—but what causes that to happen? They focus on making the teacher better but fail to understand how the student learns. If the teacher improves but the student still fails, is the system any more useful?

Innovators and entrepreneurs skilled at causal structures see the many layers to the problem—empathetic perspective—and they have a framework to see cause and effect which allows them to connect the dots between teachers, students, administrators, and parents. Causal structures are about seeing supply and demand, understanding the different perspectives, and connecting the dots into a causal framework.

CAUSAL STRUCTURES VERSUS CATEGORICAL MODELS

Young Bob didn't understand the difference between correlation and causation, so he would try to build categories to explain people. But people are different because of the context they're in, not because of a model they fit. There's a big difference between a causal structure and a categorical model.

Myers-Briggs is a categorical model. You take the test, and you're labeled a certain personality type; I'm an INTJ, but when the situation calls for it, I'm an ENTJ. Categorical models remove causation because they don't account for context. We are each hardwired to be a certain way, but that's not who you are in every circumstance. The needs of the situation dictate the response.

Similarly, people are labeled based on their generation: millennial, Gen X, boomer, etc. Being a millennial is not a causal mechanism. It's a phenomenon that has no outcomes. It can help describe who you are, but it's not a complete picture.

USING CAUSAL STRUCTURES TO NAVIGATE CHANGE

If I were advising my younger self today, I'd say, "Study how things change and evolve over time." Oftentimes people view the world in a static way, looking for absolute truths. You need to go from a static worldview to a dynamic worldview. How do things change over time?

For instance, I'm a male, and that's a static state for me—I will always be a male. But I was once a kid, then I became a student

turned engineer; I was once single, then I married and became a
father. You need to view your innovation through time. Most people
think of truth as a constant across time, and that limits their view.

Skilled innovators and entrepreneurs know that things will
never be static; change is guaranteed. That's why part of learning to
innovate must include causal structures so that you have a mechanism to respond to change. You won't always know what's going to
happen next, but having a framework to help you navigate change is
key. When your approach is static, you can't figure out how to move
and adjust. People skilled at causal structures are comfortable in the
messy middle; they can operate in a very conceptual way. And they
don't spend a lot of time worrying about right or wrong because
they are making decisions from an empathetic perspective: how
would Bob view this? Then they're applying this perspective to their
set of frameworks to help them make progress.

MAKING IT REAL

Let's compare young Bob with enlightened Bob again.

3. CAUSAL STRUCTURES

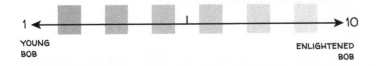

1 ←————————————————————→ 10
YOUNG
BOB
ENLIGHTENED
BOB

Young Bob would think about how something should work
almost in isolation. It would be a theoretical understanding. I'd then
solve problems by going in search of their causes and eliminating
them to make the system work—whack-a-mole. I was overly confident in how things worked, and I did not consider variation. Then
despite working in the lab, it would fail in the real world, and I'd
blame the real world.

Whereas enlightened Bob knows that he needs to understand the entire system and prepare for real word variations. So I take into account noise factors as I design. Now when problems arise, I'm prepared; I know how my thing will react. The goal for enlightened Bob is robustness. I try to make things fail as opposed to waiting for it to happen like young Bob; I want to know its limits.

Ultimately, causal structures are the magic amulet that's allowed me to work across a variety of industries successfully, everything from the space shuttle main engine to mac 'n' cheese to messaging systems and educational curriculum. Causal structures are the foundation of everything to me—a fundamental fractal. It's the underpinning piece of how I think about everything. Thank you, mentors!

Here are some ways to advance causal structures:

- Look at a task at home that seems fairly simple, and take the time to understand how it really works through using the systems diagram, such as washing the car, mowing the lawn, or baking cookies. Draw the systems diagram above, and plug in each of the components, inputs, system (action), outputs, and outcomes.

- Now practice mapping out a task at work or in the community using the systems diagram as well.

Now here are some resources to help continue your education into causal structures:

- *Principles of Systems* by Jay Wright Forrester

- *The Fifth Discipline: The Art & Practice of the Learning Organization* by Peter M. Senge

- *How to Fly a Horse: The Secret History of Creation, Invention, and Discovery* by Kevin Ashton

- *The Innovator's Dilemma: When New Technologies Cause Great Firms to Fail* by Clayton Christensen

- *The Innovator's Solution: Creating and Sustaining Successful Growth* by Clayton Christensen

- *Out of the Crisis* by W. Edwards Deming

- *Introduction to Quality Engineering: Designing Quality into Products and Processes* by Genichi Taguchi

The essence of causal structures is about being curious and understanding how things work. Once you have that perspective, you need to ask yourself, "How do I play with this thing?" That's prototyping to learn, our next chapter.

But first, let me introduce Dr. W. Edwards Deming, someone who taught me a great deal about causal structures.

THE FATHER OF
QUALITY MANAGEMENT

Meet
DR. WILLIAM EDWARDS DEMING

I first met Deming shortly before my internship at the car manufacturer in 1985. It felt random at the time, although today I don't believe in randomness. I was at an event that he attended and sat down next to him, and we talked. When the conversation began, I didn't have any idea who he was. I think I asked him fifty-two questions in twenty minutes. At the end of the conversation, he turned to me and said, "You're a curious kid. What are you doing this summer?" That's how I initially got that summer internship at the car giant; Deming was a consultant there and recommended me for the role.

Deming was a statistician and widely considered the father of quality management. He got that reputation for the work he did rebuilding the Japanese infrastructure after World War II. In the process, he pioneered methods and tools still widely used today, including total quality management. His work in Japan was so impactful that the emperor of Japan created an award in his name that is still given today to individuals or companies that make Japan a better place. I met Deming when he was at the very end of his career advising US companies.

When I eventually went to work under him, my education into how to build and launch new products began. Deming was a big proponent of case studies; he believed there was no equivalent to hands-on learning to help people understand the things that needed to happen for a solution to come about. For him, it was always about the application as opposed to the theory.

I thought of Deming as a teacher and a mentor, and while he was a pivotal person in my education, I'm not sure that he would even remember my name if he were alive today; it wasn't a personal relationship. In fact, I was a little intimidated by him. He was eighty-five and hard of hearing, so whenever he spoke to me, he screamed at me. The whole time, I didn't realize that he was deaf and hard of hearing. I thought he was just screaming at me because I wasn't doing it right.

He'd yell, "Don't ever confuse correlation with causation." And I'd think, "Okay, okay. I'm sorry."

He had a saying called SIPOC, which stood for supplier, input, process, output, and customer. He'd talk about how there's a difference between the output of something—the metric which you measure—and the outcome—the desired result. For instance, when Amrita bought the Peloton, she wanted an outcome of fitting into more clothes, but the output would be the time and effort she put into riding the bike to get that result. When we only measure outputs, we don't know if it relates to the outcomes that people seek. His goal was to help people, so even though he talked a great deal about statistics, he was actually more about empowering workers.

CHAPTER FIVE

PROTOTYPING TO LEARN

"There are way more unknowns that knowns in the universe. Our job as innovators is to discover the unknowns, make them known, and use it to build products that satisfy consumers economically."

—**Dr. Genichi Taguchi**

Many years ago, I was brought on as an advisor at a major cookie and cracker manufacturer. My job was to help them speed up their production line for two popular cookies, but as I rolled up my sleeves and got to work, people kept saying, "You should visit the chip guy; he's struggling with an issue." So I went over to see if I could help.

"I'm just having a little fragility problem—they break too easily," he told me as he brushed aside my assistance. "I'm redesigning the formula, and I just have to run one more test to confirm it, then we'll be ready to go."

"Okay," I said. But about six weeks later, people started prodding me again: "You really need to visit the chip guy." So once again, I went over to see if I could help.

"What seems to be the problem?" I asked.

"Well, I fixed the fragility problem, but now it's too thick, and the crunch went away when you bite into it, so I'm fixing that now; I almost have it, just one more test," he told me as he sent me away.

Now fast-forward six months and, guess what: the chip guy was still struggling. After hundreds of tests, he was still no closer to a solution; every time he solved one problem, he just created another. Remind you of someone? It reminded me of young Bob trying to fix the rearview mirror all those years ago, and I felt for the man. I would be so euphoric each time I thought I'd solved the problem and then equally as miserable when a new problem emerged.

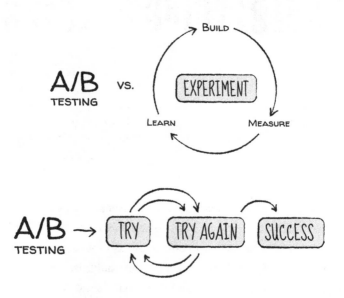

WITHOUT CAUSALITY OR WHY/HOW (JUST EFFECT)

I couldn't solve the rearview mirror problem all those years ago because I wasn't thinking about it broadly enough: In my mind, it was one problem, one solution, and therefore, I focused on the humidity rather than the system as a whole. The chip guy had fallen into the same trap. When you don't look at a situation broadly enough, you conduct A/B testing—testing one factor, then another, and so on. You are always one prototype away from solving the problem, but you never get any closer to the solution.

Rather than frame the problem and search for the solution like a needle in a haystack, you need to look at the problem as a system. What are the systems that are not performing the way that they should? Then you need to unpack those systems into control factors and noise factors?

By the time the chip guy and I sat down, he had already conducted almost three hundred samples (or experiments, I would like to say). He never planned to do so many, only one more. Together we prototyped using an orthogonal array, testing less than twenty samples that strategically represented a space of thousands of possibilities, not trying to find the answer, but trying to understand how it worked: what were the limits of the current system and the tradeoffs we needed to make? Ultimately, we solved the problem in just weeks, offering up a process and recipe that could be launched in multiple plants faster than any product before.

That's the power of prototyping to learn. You figure out how something works in context, where it doesn't work—its failure points and its limitations—and then use that knowledge to synthesize and optimize a solution that meets the desired performance and tradeoffs.

HOW DO YOU PROTOTYPE TO LEARN?

Let's break down the process of prototyping to learn by walking through a project I worked on designing dish soap for a company operating out of a developing country. The company had been developing the soap for about a year, and they were stuck; every time they got a status update from the chemists, they'd hear the same thing: "We're almost there, just one more thing to fix." And each time they'd fix the problem, something else would break.

"How many prototypes have you built?" I asked at our first meeting.

"Oh, not that many, maybe a hundred throughout the whole year," they said.

"So what did you learn?" I asked.

"We don't know why it's not working," they said, exasperated. Then they started to list the litany of issues that they'd run into, including costs. Now let's be clear. I didn't know what to do; I knew nothing about dish soap, but I had a step-by-step process for approaching problems just like this one. Here's a broad overview:

1. **System Design:** Figure out how to make it work at the lowest possible cost.

2. **Prioritization of Systems:** What are the critical systems and subsystems that drive overall performance and cost? What are the tradeoffs we need to make?

3. **Functionality of Systems:** What are the things that I can change?

4. **Measurement:** How can I use an orthogonal array to help me build an efficient set of prototypes that will maximize learning?

SYSTEM DESIGN

How does dish soap work? What's its job people are hiring it to do? Obviously, dish soap cleans dishes; that's not what I mean. I needed to figure out how dish soap does the job of cleaning dishes. What's the mechanism by which the soap works? And how does the customer know it's working?

So I learned about the cleaning system, which involves surfactants that attack both fat and carbohydrates, breaking them down into smaller pieces. Then I realized that the soap needed to create foam. Without foam, the customer wouldn't get the feedback that it's working. You can actually make dish soap without foam that does an excellent job of cleaning, but people won't realize it's cleaning and keep adding more and more soap. I also found that the majority of people use dish soap with a sponge; therefore, if it's too thin, the soap runs straight through the sponge and down the drain. Next, I needed to consider smell and color. Finally, the dish soap needed to do all of these jobs while staying within a competitive cost structure.

As you lay out all the systems, you suddenly realize that there are six different functions for dish soap.

PRIORITIZATION OF SYSTEMS

Now I needed to prioritize those functions. What are the critical systems that drive overall performance and cost? For instance, the fragrance and color are fairly independent and not where you'll spend a lot of time and money. However, the bubbles, thickness, and cleaning system are critical components.

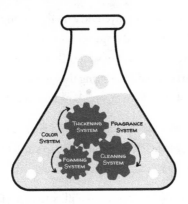

FUNCTIONALITY OF SYSTEMS

Next, I broke down those functions into parameters with control factors and noise factors. How could I change the things that I had control over to make me less sensitive to the things I couldn't control? How could I set the control factors so that the noise factors no longer affected the output?

The dish soap would be used in a developing country where there's both hard and soft water. Therefore, we needed to create a dish soap that worked in both scenarios. Most people don't even know what kind of water they have, so you can't create and sell dish soap based on water type. Additionally, the detergent had to work on very greasy foods like olive oil, and on carbohydrates—like rice that gets caked onto pots and pans. These were all noise factors that influenced the system.

We needed to play with the chemical makeup of the cleaning mechanism, our control factor, to determine how it impacted the outputs in the system: foam, thickness, etc.

MEASUREMENT

Now it was time to build a method for measuring the critical systems:

- To test the foam, we invented a method using a George Foreman grill where I put a specific amount of dish soap on the grill with a set amount of water. Then I would measure how many times I needed to wring the sponge in the grill before the soap started to foam and how long that foam lasted.

- We measured the thickness of the soap in a tube and then looked at the length of time the soap stuck to the top of the sponge rather than just running through it.

- We also measured the soap's ability to break fat and carbohydrates into particle size.

Then I played with the chemical formula. There were different actives in the surfactants, so as I adjusted the percent of actives, I looked at the impact on the overall cleaning mechanism as well as changes to foaming and thickness. I knew that I did not have control over the context in which the customer would use the soap, so those were the noise factors that I tested each of the control factors against.

- Hard versus soft water
- Hot water versus cool water
- Grease versus caked food

Once I understood how many factors I was playing with, I knew how many tests I needed to run by simply plugging the numbers into one of Dr. Genichi Taguchi's arrays from his book *Taguchi Methods: Orthogonal Arrays and Linear Graphs*. These arrays allow me to measure multiple factors simultaneously and understand how a thing works over sets of tests, within sets of conditions: the opposite of A/B testing or solving one problem at a time. And the tests are fully balanced. With the dish soap, for instance, nine tests were performed with the color yellow, and nine with blue. We didn't expect the color to have any impact at all, but as it turns out, blue is an oil-based color and yellow is a water-based color. Therefore, the blue didn't work as well because the surfactant used some of its power to break down the color rather than clean the greasy dishes.

As you can see, the key to this approach was that it did not rely on my theory of what the "best" dish soap was. I had no idea how the experiments were going to turn out; I let the dish soap tell me which one was the best. It was based entirely on empirical data.

We ended up building eighteen prototypes that we measured against all these different dimensions, which answered a ton of questions: How well did it stay on the sponge? How well did it cut grease? If the water was dirty, did it still foam? What was the foam height? What was the cost? By the end, I had a whole understanding about what made the best dish soap. For instance, I knew that when I increased the magnesium chloride, it increased foam height without adding to the cost, but it made the soap thinner. Prototyping to learn allows me to see these tradeoffs.

Whenever I prototype, I know that some things are going to work, and others will not, but all of it helps me learn. Too often, people get singularly focused: "I want to make a dish soap with the most foam." Prototyping will show which dish soap has the best foam, but it will also detail tradeoffs like cost. You start to realize that you can't make the "best" soap because you will lose money. You are able to make the tradeoffs in real time.

APPLYING PROTOTYPING

I created a detailed link for this chapter that demonstrates prototyping to learn, with a catapult like the experiment from the Introduction: learningtobuildbook.com. Let's walk through it...

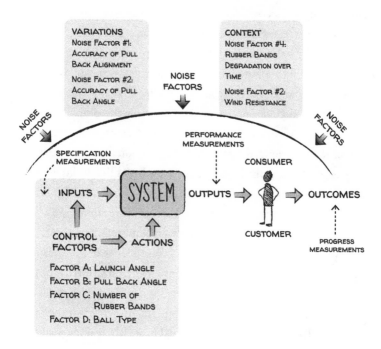

Think of the orthogonal array as the magic square that allows me to test a wide variation of conditions without having to test everything. We need to look at the system design and identify the control factors. For the catapult, that includes launch angle, pull-back angle, number of rubber bands, and ball type. Then there are the noise factors, which include the precision of use—meaning if the pull-back angle is thirty degrees, the user may only do twenty-nine. We are going to plug our control factors into our orthogonal array and use the noise factors to create variation.

Below is the orthogonal array, or magic square, that prescribes what nine prototypes to make.

DESIGNED EXPERIMENT L9(3⁴)				
PROTOTYPE NUMBER	FACTOR A	FACTOR B	FACTOR C	FACTOR D
1	1	1	1	1
2	1	2	2	2
3	1	3	3	3
4	2	1	2	3
5	2	2	3	1
6	2	3	1	2
7	3	1	3	2
8	3	2	1	3
9	3	3	2	1

FACTOR	LAUNCH ANGLE	NUMBER OF RUBBER BANDS	PULL BACK ANGLE	BALL TYPE
LEVEL 1	30	3 BANDS	45	WIFFLE
LEVEL 2	45	2 BANDS	60	YELLOW
LEVEL 3	60	1 BAND	75	WHITE

CONTROL FACTORS				
PROTOTYPE NUMBER	LAUNCH ANGLE	NUMBER OF RUBBER BANDS	PULL BACK ANGLE	BALL TYPE
1	30	3 BANDS	45	WIFFLE
2	30	2 BANDS	60	YELLOW
3	30	1 BAND	75	WHITE
4	45	3 BANDS	60	WHITE
5	45	2 BANDS	75	WIFFLE
6	45	1 BAND	45	YELLOW
7	60	3 BANDS	75	YELLOW
8	60	2 BANDS	45	WHITE
9	60	1 BAND	60	WIFFLE

My goal is to design a robust catapult that consistently delivers results. To do this, I add the noise factors as I shoot the ball and measure the different distances. Now I'm going to set up the catapult and just shoot it. I'm not trying to figure out how to make it go a certain distance at this point; I just want to learn how the catapult works in the face of noise. Then I get the average distance, the variation of distance, and the signal-to-noise ratio, a measure of robustness.

PROTOTYPE NUMBER	CONTROL FACTORS			
	LAUNCH ANGLE	NUMBER OF RUBBER BANDS	PULL BACK ANGLE	BALL TYPE
1	30	3 BANDS	45	WIFFLE
2	30	2 BANDS	60	YELLOW
3	30	1 BAND	75	WHITE
4	45	3 BANDS	60	WHITE
5	45	2 BANDS	75	WIFFLE
6	45	1 BAND	45	YELLOW
7	60	3 BANDS	75	YELLOW
8	60	2 BANDS	45	WHITE
9	60	1 BAND	60	WIFFLE

OUTPUTS (DISTANCE)	NOISE FACTORS (DISTANCE)			
	OVER PULL RIGHT	UNDER PULL RIGHT	OVER PULL LEFT	UNDER PULL LEFT
1	214	214	224	206
2	162	144	138	135
3	100	98	94	79
4	182	184	184	178
5	270	272	259	251
6	82	79	81	75
7	115	114	116	113
8	120	124	117	94
9	101	104	99	95

ANALYSIS	AVERAGE DISTANCE	DISTANCE VARIANCE	S/N RATIO (ROBUSTNESS)	COST
1	215	54.33	29.28	3.75
2	145	146.25	21.55	4.5
3	93	90.25	19.78	3.75
4	182	8.00	36.17	4.25
5	263	96.67	28.54	3.5
6	79	9.58	28.16	4.25
7	115	1.67	38.96	4.75
8	114	181.58	18.51	4
9	100	14.25	28.44	3.25

Ultimately, once I have that data, how do I look at these things? I break it down into three critical factors:

- What changes the average distance?
- What improves the robustness of the distance?
- How do I understand the cost aspect?

ANALYSIS

	CONTROL FACTORS				ANALYSIS		
PROTOTYPE NUMBER	LAUNCH ANGLE	NUMBER OF RUBBER BANDS	PULL BACK ANGLE	BALL TYPE	AVERAGE DISTANCE	S/N RATIO (ROBUSTNESS)	COST
1	1	1	1	1	215	29.28	$3.75
2	1	2	2	2	145	21.55	$4.50
3	1	3	3	3	93	19.78	$4.25
4	2	1	2	3	182	36.17	$4.25
5	2	2	3	1	263	28.54	$3.50
6	2	3	1	2	79	28.16	$4.25
7	3	1	3	2	115	38.96	$4.75
8	3	2	1	3	114	18.51	$4.00
9	3	3	2	1	100	28.44	$3.25

FACTOR	LAUNCH ANGLE	NUMBER OF RUBBER BANDS	PULL BACK ANGLE	BALL TYPE
LEVEL 1	30	3 BANDS	45	WIFFLE
LEVEL 2	45	2 BANDS	60	YELLOW
LEVEL 3	60	1 BANDS	75	WHITE

AVERAGE DISTANCE

FACTOR	LAUNCH ANGLE	NUMBER OF RUBBER BANDS	PULL BACK ANGLE	BALL TYPE
LEVEL 1	150.67	170.33	135.83	192.42
LEVEL 2	174.75	173.83	142.17	112.83
LEVEL 3	109.33	90.58	156.75	129.50
DIFF	65.42	83.25	20.92	79.58
RANK	3	1	4	2

S/N RATIO (ROBUSTNESS)

FACTOR	LAUNCH ANGLE	NUMBER OF RUBBER BANDS	PULL BACK ANGLE	BALL TYPE
LEVEL 1	23.54	34.80	25.32	28.75
LEVEL 2	30.96	22.87	28.72	29.56
LEVEL 3	28.64	25.46	29.09	24.82
DIFF	7.42	11.93	3.78	4.74
RANK	2	1	4	3

COST

FACTOR	LAUNCH ANGLE	NUMBER OF RUBBER BANDS	PULL BACK ANGLE	BALL TYPE
LEVEL 1	23.54	34.80	25.32	28.75
LEVEL 2	30.96	22.87	28.72	29.56
LEVEL 3	28.64	25.46	29.09	24.82
DIFF	7.42	11.93	3.78	4.74
RANK	2	1	4	3

Pretty quickly, I learn a few things.

- The launch angle, for instance, affects consistency a lot. Some settings make the ball travel very high, vertical almost, and then the ball is pulled back down by gravity, causing it to travel a shorter distance, while other settings cause the ball to travel on a more horizontal path. The relationship between the launch angle and distance is not linear here because the bigger angles cause the ball to go high instead of straight.

- Pull-back angle has more linear results: if I pull it back less, it's going to go shorter; if I pull it back more, it's going to travel farther. The results are very predictable.

- There's a big difference between one rubber band and two, but only a small improvement from two to three, and each rubber band adds cost.

- The Wiffle ball has holes, so it reduces wind drag the best because the air passes right through it rather than knocking the ball off course. On average, the Wiffle ball travels more than 50 percent farther.

You quickly realize that what causes the catapult to be robust—consistent in the face of noise factors—is different than what causes it to travel a certain distance. The launch angle is more important to consistency than anything else because you do not want the high arches; you want the ball to travel horizontally. By locking that launch angle and playing with the pull-back angle, your results will be more consistent, but you may have to settle for the ball traveling a shorter distance.

Now let's factor in costs. In this scenario, each rubber band costs $0.25. Additionally, we are experimenting with three different ball types: the Wiffle ball costs $0.50, the white ball costs $1.00, and the yellow ball costs $1.50.

Ultimately, you now know how the settings impact distance, consistency, and cost. Now you can decide how to make tradeoffs—the next chapter.

This goes back to the red line/green line story from Chapter 1. On the red line, we would make one design and see how it worked, while on the green line, they would make nine designs to understand the entire system and then dial it back. Then down the road, when the green line innovators ran into problems, they knew what to change because they understood how the system worked. Conversely, the red line innovators would start testing one factor at a time to solve the problem. On the green line, you know what's important—like the catapult launch angle—and what you can play with. You're not optimizing in a vacuum for one performance attribute but rather seeing the tradeoffs. In the end, this allows you to build the best thing without sacrificing quality or cost.

THE PROBLEM WITH RELYING ON A HYPOTHESIS

Most people don't prototype to learn; they prototype to confirm a hypothesis with A/B testing. Why? Because we're taught that we should already have the answer based on theory. As engineers, we're taught that we have an expertise in a certain vertical—electrical engineering, mechanical engineering, etc.—and therefore, we think in terms of content. With this mindset, you look at a problem and believe that you should have the answer based on your knowledge base. Therefore, you assume certain knowns and run experiments based on theoretical knowledge. You think that you only need to change one factor. It's a false notion.

Theory alone only gets you to a certain point; it's relative to context. When you build on theory and problems arise, you focus on trying to change the context rather than looking at the system and asking, "What are the systems that are not performing the way that they should?" Prototyping to learn is not about confirming a theory or hypothesis. It's about empirically getting to the limits of theory to understand how to build better. You're pushing the limits of your thing, and therefore, you know where it fails. You're not surprised like young Bob with the rearview mirror.

Most people say, "I think it works this way; let's test and see if I'm right." I never feel smart enough to do that. I'm actually using experiments to help me form my hypotheses as opposed to relying on theory from the past. "Let's just play with it and see what it does," I say. It's about being humble enough to know that you don't know. My insecurities are an asset; they help me build the right questions, test the right things. While most people are trying to prove the output, I'm trying to understand what outputs my inputs even create. From there, I deduce how it works. Ultimately, building a very specific theory of how this system works in this condition.

I'm not advocating throwing theory out the window but acknowledging that theory only gets you in the game; it's the minor leagues because it's based in the past. You need present, empirical data to innovate for the future.

WHAT MAKES THE BEST INNOVATORS?

In school, I was taught that to be an innovator, you needed to be the smartest, most knowledgeable person in the room on a particular subject. Great innovators had depth of knowledge. But over time, I realized that experts were overly biased, and it actually got in the way of innovation because it caused them to assume aspects were understood to a greater extent than the reality. The truth is that there's more unknown on almost any subject than is known.

Ultimately, I've found that the key to successful innovation is not a solid base knowledge on the subject matter. Instead, successful innovation requires thinking, methods, tools, and frameworks for framing problems, experimenting, and designing solutions, combined with hard work. In the book *How to Fly a Horse*, Kevin Ashton concludes that those who are humble, experiment and learn, and have an incredible work ethic—reps as I say—are some of the keys.

Part of what made Taguchi, Deming, and Moore so successful—all PhDs—was their humbleness to know that they did not know.

THE LIMITS OF THEORY

As a young engineer, I had the good fortune to learn prototyping from a master like Taguchi. He used to tell a story that underscored the importance of prototyping to learn and the limits of existing theory...

For one hundred years, tile manufacturers everywhere struggled to produce uniform tiles. By the 1950s, they'd largely reached the point where they accepted the problem as unchangeable. But Taguchi set out to test that theory.

First, he went to the production line to figure out how the system worked. The tiles came out of the kiln by the thousands, went down the production line, and were stacked into enormous piles to use the space efficiently. As the tiles dried in the kiln, the ones sitting on the outside of the pile dried faster, shrank, and got brittle, causing them to crack easily. The tiles in the center couldn't drive off the moisture well, and therefore wouldn't shrink as much and cracked. Because of this, tile manufacturers couldn't produce uniform tiles, which led to a major sorting endeavor after each day's run, involving scores of people who grouped the tiles into three to four size categories.

So Taguchi looked at the control factors and noise factors. How could he design an experiment that changed the things he had control over so that the tiles would be less sensitive to the context in which they dried? He began by experimenting with the kiln: What distance did the tiles travel? What temperatures were they subjected to? How fast did the temperatures ramp up and down? How long did they hold temperatures? Taguchi found that by playing with the kiln alone, he was able to solve the problem that had plagued tile manufacturers for one hundred years. They never had to sort again. This not only solved the size issue but also increased capacity threefold.

It underscores the power of obtaining present, empirical data—prototyping to learn—as opposed to relying on past theory. The problem with relying on existing theory alone is that it causes you to assume certain aspects are known.

ACCEPTING THE UNKNOWNS

There's way more unknown than known in this world! Successful innovators and entrepreneurs have humility; they know that they don't know, and as a result, they use prototyping to learn. This series of tweets from @etiennefd in Montreal perfectly encapsulates this notion of the unknown:

> Sometimes I think of how cakes are a miracle. Take a pound cake: it's made of equal amounts (one pound each) of four ingredients.
>
> Sounds simple, right?

To get the first ingredient, you need to find some species of grass that grows in the Middle East.

When the grass is ripe and golden, you harvest the greens. Then you grind them to get a fine powder. You remove the darker parts of the powder to just keep the white.

That was the easiest ingredient. You'll need another plant: a large grass that grows in tropical areas.

The part you need is some sweet juice in the stocks. After a lot of labor-intensive processing and refining, you turn this juice into thousands of tiny white crystals.

You're not done yet. For the next ordeal, you must hunt this flightless bird from the jungles of Asia. Don't kill it though. Just take the weird round things the females lay.

Crack the weird round thing open: it's slimy and fat and bright yellow. That's exactly what you want.

The last one's tough. You need the female of this massive (but peaceful) beast. You need it to have just given birth. You need to take the white liquid it wanted to give its baby.

Then you need to extract the fat from that liquid, and mix it until it becomes a yellowish solid.

Now combine these four things in a very specific order before you apply a very specific amount of heat for a very specific amount of time, and you have a pound cake!

Maybe you'd like to add some flavor?

Perhaps the tiny fragrant seeds of an expensive orchid?

Or the bitter processed fat from a Central American fruit?

Or the dried bark from some tree in India?

Maybe we shouldn't get too fancy...

The reason cakes exist, of course, is that we had centuries to domesticate plants and animals, and to create culinary innovations.

Complex things can come into being, with time and mechanisms like culture or natural selection.

But make no mistake: cakes are a miracle.

—**Étienne Fortier-Dubois**

As you go through time, a poundcake seems simple, but it's taken knowledge, experience, and evolution through innovation to make a poundcake easy—a lot of innovation. It is humbling to know all the people and time it took to make something "easy." Nothing becomes easy without struggles, experiments, knowledge, and a lot of hard work. Now think of the world at large. There are so many possibilities, so many unknowns; we still have a lot more to do. That's why prototyping to learn is so important, everything evolves over time; we just need to find the next evolution. Prototyping creates possibilities.

Innovators and entrepreneurs should be doing a lot more prototyping. In foresight, A/B testing looks easier and faster, but in hindsight, it's actually longer and less effective. Taguchi would always say, "A/B testing is job security for engineers." It's a shotgun approach where you throw everything at the wall and see what sticks. The problem: you don't understand where your thing fails; you can't see around corners, so it's like building on a house of cards; it will ultimately collapse in the long term. It's simplicity on the wrong side of complexity because it's not based on a sound understanding of how something works.

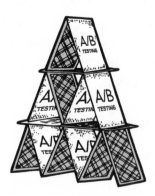

Successful innovators and entrepreneurs understand that they need to frame and build around knowns, and they are humble enough to know that they don't know. Therefore, they use prototyping to help them discover what works.

MAKING IT REAL

Let's compare young Bob with enlightened Bob again.

4. PROTOTYPING TO LEARN

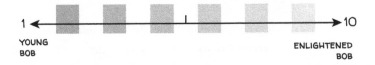

1 ←   → 10

YOUNG
BOB

ENLIGHTENED
BOB

Young Bob is an A/B tester. I build a house of cards that works in the lab but is not robust. I narrow things down, hold one thing constant, and change one factor at a time, but I don't understand how the whole system works. I'm a hypothesis builder who uses the scientific method, and I incrementally move forward one step at a time.

Enlightened Bob, however, takes a step back and sees the larger perspective. I might know in theory how my thing works, but I know that I need to let the system tell me, not theory. I'm humble enough to know that I don't know, so I find the limits of my thing by causing problems early in the design. Ultimately, young Bob is trying to find the answer, while enlightened Bob is trying to understand how it works in the real world.

Now think about your product, and ask yourself a few questions:

- How do I frame the system and the boundaries of the system?

- How do I break that down into control factors and noise factors?

- How do I use an orthogonal array to let it tell me how it works?

Now here are some resources to help continue your education into prototyping to learn:

- *Prototyping: A Practitioner's Guide* by Todd Zaki Warfel.

- *Product Design and Development* by Karl Ulrich and Steven D. Eppinger.

- *Total Quality Development: A Step-By-Step Guide to World-Class Concurrent Engineering* by Don Clausing.

- *Taguchi Methods Orthogonal Arrays and Linear Graphs: Tools for Quality Engineering* by Dr. Genichi Taguchi.

- *Ten Types of Innovation: The Discipline of Building Break-throughs* by Larry Keeley, Ryan Pikkel, Brian Quinn, and Helen Walters

- *Serious Play: How the World's Best Companies Simulate to Innovate* by Michael Schrage

- *Change by Design: How Design Thinking Transforms Organizations and Inspires Innovation* by Tim Brown

When prototyping, there's never just one answer. There are always tradeoffs. Optimization at its essence is about a series of tradeoffs, which leads us into our next chapter, *Making Tradeoffs*.

But first, let me introduce Dr. Genichi Taguchi, probably the best that there's ever been when it comes to prototyping to learn.

Meet
DR. GENICHI TAGUCHI

I met Dr. Genichi Taguchi during that first internship at the car manufacturer. He was in his sixties; I was all of twenty. I was the person in the front row asking all the questions while everyone else remained silent: "Wait a second. I don't understand…" As a result, he knew exactly who I was because everyone else was either afraid to question him or thought it was not appropriate to do so. Instead, Taguchi loved my questions, and it solidified our relationship.

Taguchi was the equivalent of the Dalai Lama for innovation in my opinion. He was smart in a practical way. People would tell him he couldn't do something, and he'd figure out a way; he'd take a pair of pliers and use them as a hammer. People would say, "You can't do that." But suddenly, the pliers became not just a hammer but a better hammer. He was resourceful.

Learning from Taguchi was the beginning of night vision goggles for me. He taught me how to form questions so that I could get to intent, then take that intent and turn it into action. For instance, when you drive a car, you may have the intent to turn, but that intent starts in your head. It's the action of turning the wheel that brings your intent to life. Taguchi would say that if you talk to most people about turning a car, they'd say you need a steering wheel, but without a steering wheel, we might be able to innovate four hundred other ways to turn a car. His point was that the consumers' intent was way more important than knowing how they wanted their steering wheel built. "Don't get caught up in the solution; get caught up in the problem consumers have," he'd say. "A well-framed consumer problem is ten times easier to solve than a solution looking for a problem."

Taguchi was always obsessed with measurement. He would say, "How do you make something better if you can't measure the variation?" He believed that all innovation must start with better measurement—and measurement of the "right" things. He would always tell me, "You're measuring the wrong thing; you're not thinking about this right." When we were painting the cars, it was about reducing rework. He'd say, "You've got to measure the functional thing that's not happening. Where's the variation?" This would force me to go down to the right level. I learned the importance and utility of metrics and structure.

I worked side by side with Taguchi from 1985 to 1991 at the car manufacturer. Then again for several more years on two other projects.

CHAPTER SIX

MAKING TRADEOFFS

"You're better off with a kick-ass half than a half-assed whole."

—**Jason Fried**, Entrepreneur, CEO and co-founder of Basecamp

Tradeoffs are one of the keys to making progress. You must be able to define what you are willing to give up to move forward. I think of tradeoffs as, you can have it *this* way; you can have it *that* way; or you cannot have it at all. As innovators and entrepreneurs, we never have enough time, money, or knowledge to make it perfect. Perfection is the trap, progress is the true measure, and tradeoffs are the way to get there. But like everything, knowing how to frame them to get the data and knowledge is the challenge.

For instance, I'm working on a dating app, and during interviews, I talked to an impressive woman in her early thirties—Harvard law degree, employed at a big Washington, DC law firm—who was struggling to find a partner. As we talked, I realized the problem: she couldn't make tradeoffs. She saw the dating pool as infinite, and therefore just kept swiping, looking for the perfect match. "I don't want to settle," she told me. But she failed to realize that nobody's perfect; marriage is about helping each other, and a set of acceptable compromises.

People struggle with tradeoffs when they view them as settling. Tradeoffs are not about settling; they are about making progress by determining what's most important. When you can't make tradeoffs, you get stuck in decision hell, trying to find the proverbial needle in the haystack.

Look back to the catapult. By having all the data, we could actually frame the tradeoffs so that we could make way better decisions. By knowing how it worked and having the empirical data, we could make the tradeoffs to have it perform better and more consistently at a lower cost.

WHY TRADEOFFS MATTER FOR INNOVATORS AND ENTREPRENEURS

When Basecamp first started to think about an app for the phone, they initially tried to put everything in it to replicate their web-based platform. Then they realized that it made the app way too slow on the phone. So they asked themselves, "What are the types of things people would do on the phone versus the computer?" You're not going to create a new account or a new project on your phone. But you will respond to comments and check your lists. So they stripped the app down to the point where it does only the things you might do while standing in line at the grocery store or taking the train home from work.

When the app was packed full and too slow, people downloaded it but never used it. Now usage has skyrocketed because they managed tradeoffs. They recognized that they couldn't have everything, so they only kept what was most important—a kick-ass half.

Tradeoffs are just as much about cost as functionality. What's good enough?

> "Cost is more important than quality, but quality is the best way to reduce cost."
>
> —**Genichi Taguchi**

Taguchi used to talk about how Mercedes had it easy because they made their specifications so tight; everything fit perfectly. But the reality is, to make it perfect, you've got to build ten parts and throw away nine, dramatically increasing costs. It's like French cooking: If you use a lot of high-quality ingredients, it's hard to make a bad thing. Skilled innovators and entrepreneurs can take a product that's not perfect and make something great out of it by making the right tradeoffs. Thereby reducing costs while maintaining enough quality.

The red line/green line story from Chapter 1 is a perfect example of the power in managing tradeoffs well. When I compared the systems of the American design to the Japanese design, the American one was superior on a microscopic level. Take the exhaust system, for example: each component used to build our version was higher quality, but when I compared the two exhaust systems side by side in their entirety, the Japanese version outperformed, and it did so at half the cost. Innovators and entrepreneurs skilled at managing tradeoffs understand this complexity. And as a result, they frame tradeoffs within the context of the whole system. What's the economic impact of failure? For instance, one screw falling out is not a big deal. A hundred screws, on the other hand, now that's a big deal.

Tradeoffs are the key to great decision-making. It's critical to being a good consumer and even more critical to becoming a skilled innovator and entrepreneur. You can't have it all, so you must look at the totality, understand how it's interconnected, and determine what's good enough.

TOOLS FOR LEARNING TO MANGE TRADEOFFS

There are a couple of tricks I employ that force me to see tradeoffs and thereby swiftly move me through the design process:

- Setting constraints

- Seeing the big picture

SETTING CONSTRAINTS

One of the keys to forcing tradeoffs in innovation, as well as selling, is a time wall or a time box. A time wall can be artificial, or not, but it's the fabricated notion that you must complete something by a certain date. If there's no time wall, you might innovate forever rather than bring your thing to market. But the moment a time wall is established, it forces you to make tradeoffs. What's most important? What's least important? It sets your priorities. It's a triangulation between time, cost, and quality. No one can have it all! A time wall pushes you to decide rather than endlessly tweak and expand your thing. Think of an hourglass: it's always running out of time.

When innovating, I give myself what I call a time box: I have *this* much time, to do *that* much work. After I set the time box, I shape the work to fit into that box. When you innovate without a time box, you end up continually playing with your thing, adding on features and benefits. As a result, you fail to make explicit tradeoffs. When you hold the time box constant, you give yourself a time wall that puts pressure on the situation. It allows you to see what's really important.

The Value of Time

Many years ago, on my departure after traveling to Japan to meet with Dr. Taguchi, he bowed down before me and presented me with a beautiful Seiko watch as a gift. At the time, I was just a young man in my twenties, Taguchi a sixty-five-year-old success story, and I will never forget the words that he spoke to me that day...

"I'm giving you this watch because at my age, I've learned that the most precious of all resources is time. You need to manage your time even better than you manage your money. Don't let anyone steal your time because you can never get it back. When you look at this watch, I hope it reminds you to spend your time wisely, making the world a better place."

The power of that sentiment resonates with me more every single day.

Many years ago, I decided to expand the notion of a time wall to my life expectancy. You see, I'd recently conducted interviews with industry leaders who had emerged from out of nowhere—dark horses—and done amazing things. One of their key characteristics was that they all valued time and viewed their life as precious. Over 80 percent told me that it stemmed from a near-death experience that rocked them to their core and changed their perspective. They became more intentional in their choices and stopped putting up with crap. To outsiders, their decisiveness came across as brash and overly confident, cocky, but for them, it became the key to their success. It shaped their decision-making; they stopped wasting time.

And so I asked myself, "How do I manufacture this mindset without actually having a near-death experience?"

Immediately, I thought of my mom. She worked hard her whole life, for thirty years, as a Detroit area public schoolteacher and never really took any time to enjoy herself. "I'll do that when I retire," she'd always say. She saved all her money; she didn't vacation. Shortly after retiring at sixty-two, she received a devastating diagnosis of colon cancer and died just four months later. I saw my own mortality in her story. My mom had no idea what was coming, but I've been blessed with the foresight to realize that maybe I only have until I'm sixty-two as well.

So I picked my death date based on my mom's lifespan. Obviously, I don't really know when I'm going to die, but I know that it's possible. That means today I have less than seven years left to live. What am I going to do? What am I not going to do? By living with an expiration date, it forces me to make very conscious tradeoffs about what I'm willing to put up with, even at the simplest level. For instance, I go to two baseball games every year. If I only have seven years to live, that's fourteen more games. When I view it through that lens, I realize I don't want to see the Mariners and the Tigers; I want to see the Yankees and the Red Socks.

Creating a time wall for my life causes me to intentionally shape what I want to do. And the reality is, what do I lose if I live beyond that day? Nothing. Now I have bonus days. But by living with this mindset, I force myself to make tradeoffs, and therefore, I make better decisions. I'm not waiting until I retire to do the things that I enjoy. I do those things now. People ask me all the time, "How in the world can you write a book, work on three products, and volunteer?" But how can I not? I know what I want to accomplish in my life, and I've faced my mortality. In a hundred years, we will all be forgotten, just specs in the timeline of the universe. It's why I'm writing this book. The minimum that I can do before my time is up is pass on the knowledge that others have shared.

Another effective constraint is a dollar wall: I can't spend more than *this* amount of money to get *that* accomplished. Again, it forces you to make explicit tradeoffs by placing yet another set of constraints on your thing. The dollar wall forces you to scope the work and de-risk.

SEEING THE BIG PICTURE

Forcing yourself to view the whole so that you can see how the pieces are interconnected is another way to help manage tradeoffs. In my office, for instance, I have a room lined with boards that represent categories of work: suspects, prospects, proposals, etc. Then within each board are cards for the work within that category. It allows me to see the whole while realizing that I have a limited capacity. Therefore, I can shift my priorities and easily make tradeoffs.

So in September, I could see the number of projects coming in and subsequently how that would fill my calendar. Now the tradeoffs were clear: I was prepared to lose those clients because they needed something the next day. My online classes needed to be pushed back to satisfy incoming demand. But writing the books and building new products were a priority, so I'd only take on the new clients to the extent that it would fit that priority. It gets back to the notion of being explicit about decisions. Now when I look at my calendar, it represents the progress that I want to make. And I've made explicit tradeoffs: I want to help people, but I recognize that with the books, I can help more people, so I defer my time to that versus individual work.

This intentional mindset goes back to the time wall that I've established for my life. If I only have 2,587 days left, what do I want to do with that time? Tradeoffs become very clear when viewed from this perspective.

Playing with a set of possible scenarios is an excellent way to see the big picture. When a company comes to me for advice, I'll use this technique to help flush out potential opportunities and weaknesses:

- Imagine that I just bought you. Here's what I would do...

- If I was your competitor, what should I do?

- If I'm a startup trying to disrupt your industry, what should I do?

Similarly, when someone comes to me for help building their thing, I'll present several possible scenarios to flush out what's important:

- If I wanted that done in half the time, what would you change? How much would it cost?

- If I gave you unlimited money, what would you do? How long would it take?

- If I gave you unlimited time to make your thing perfect, how much time would you need?

Setting different types of possible scenarios forces you to think about your thing differently. Remember, you can't have it all. Do you value time or money? What's good enough? What does progress look like? It also helps you see the next iteration of your thing. Then try to think of everything as a draft; nothing is final: in the first round we do *this*, and in the second round we do *that*. You're not saying that you'll never do it; you're just prioritizing.

Most people plan horribly because they can't see the big picture; they plan for what they know, but they don't plan for the unknowns. And therefore, they are building their thing off assumptions. To see the tradeoffs, you've got to see the whole so that you can make connections, and therefore make better decisions in whatever you're trying to do. Instead of making isolated decisions and asking, "Do I do *this*, or do I do *that*?" you are now taking a step back, seeing the bigger picture, and understanding the cost, time, and performance implications of your decisions.

I have learned to plan from right to left as discussed in causal structures. Think of the left as the beginning and the right as the end. Thinking of the end first helps me frame what I don't know and what I need to do to get that knowledge. Just as my friend Ryan did in Chapter 1 when writing his book.

Successful innovators and entrepreneurs do not view tradeoffs as a compromise. Rather, they see them as necessary tools for managing the speed at which they move forward. And instead of trying to make all the progress in one step by building the "best" version, they see half steps to make progress and evolve to the solution through multiple iterations. For example, the first iPhone was not a perfect solution to begin with, but it was a better solution than the BlackBerry, and it evolved over time through multiple iterations.

When you can't see tradeoffs, you get stuck. It's like continually trying to put ten pounds of crap into a five-pound bag. Overstuffing the bag never works. You're just left with unintended consequences, where you solve one problem just to create another. Ultimately, tradeoffs are about understanding which problems you're going to care about. But you need to be able to see tradeoffs, not just from the supply-side, but from the demand-side as well.

HOW SHOULD CUSTOMERS' TRADEOFFS INFLUENCE YOUR PRODUCT?

Everyone makes tradeoffs to make progress: "I'm willing to give up *this* so I can get *that*." No one can have everything. What tradeoffs is your customer willing to make? What's most important? What's least important?

You need to be able to reflect their values and their tradeoffs in the way you make your product. Think of the dish soap example from the last chapter. I might be able to make it clean, but if it doesn't foam, customers will think it's not working. I have to opti-mize between the foam that they see and the ability to clean. To do this, I have to understand the tradeoffs between the two things. Ulti-mately, knowing how the customer is going to use it and what they are going to use it for helps me decide how much money to put into a foaming system versus the cleaning system.

For the customer, tradeoffs happen when people are in the "deciding" stage of the timeline from Chapter 3. This is where prior-ities are set and value codes are determined. It's a triangle between time, cost, and quality. No one can have it all! People set their expec-tations here and will base their satisfaction on the criteria they set.

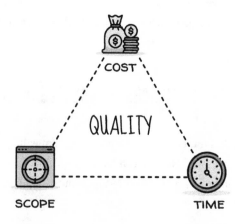

It's important that you identify the tradeoffs consumers are willing to make first. Don't talk features, benefits, and cost because people are willing to make tradeoffs. What makes your product or service kick ass? Where do you say no? Basically, choose what to suck at. This goes back to the quote at the beginning of the chapter: "You're better off with a kick-ass half than a half-assed whole."

Recently, a friend came to me and asked if I could help her get a family member unstuck during the decision-making process for buying a new condo. John had recently lost his wife and was consolidating from two homes to one. He and his wife spent half the year up north and the other half in Palm Beach, Florida. John wanted to move to Florida full-time. His children, however, worried that he didn't have any family in Palm Beach and wanted him to relocate closer to family that already lived in Florida.

Eager, John jumped into home hunting from afar as he was still settling the New York property, so his family in Florida started to preview properties on his behalf via video conferencing. Immediately, John saw a condo that he loved and made an offer. But as he waited for the seller's response, he got nervous and started to over-analyze the property: the building was too close to the one next door, and parking was too limited. When sellers tried to negotiate price, John haggled with his objections in mind and lost the sale.

Just a week later, John saw another condo that looked perfect and sent his family to go look. Again, John made an offer almost immediately, but this time, his offer was accepted. Again, he started to stress over the details: closeness to the street, security system, recycling, and pool maintenance. When the sellers refused to fix an issue with the air conditioning, John pulled out of the deal.

When he finally arrived in Florida to look in person, John saw nothing he liked; everything had at least one or two little details out of place. At this point, he'd looked with my friend at over thirty properties, and none were acceptable.

"What is he afraid of?" I asked.

Often when people can't make a choice, it's because they are afraid of something. I suspected that there was some anxiety force that was manifesting through objections.

"You need to take him out to lunch and ask what he's really afraid of," I told her. "Maybe he's unsure about relocating. You've got to attack the habit of the old."

Then I told her if it were me, I'd play a game with him: "Imagine that there are only three condos left, and these are the three condos. Which one would you pick, and why?" It would force him to make a choice, at least in a hypothetical scenario, and it would help determine what's really important to him.

Then I would take him out to view a wider range of condos, including condos he wouldn't consider buying because they were either above or below his price range. I'd let him see what it would cost to get the security features, pool maintenance, distance from the street, etc. He needed to see the tradeoff he'd make on price to get those amenities.

Finally, I would apply a time wall. It's one of the most valuable tools for framing tradeoffs. Tell John that he needed to make a decision by a certain date, December 1, because otherwise, he'd run into the holidays. Then tell him that if he couldn't decide by then, he should take a few months off and start again in the Spring when the inventory would be high. Imposing a time wall, would force him to either make the decision or not make the decision.

Consumers need help to make tradeoffs. Attacking the forces of progress—pushes, pulls, anxieties, and habits—then applying a time wall is a very effective way to help people move forward and make progress.

The key is that the previous four skills taught in this book all feed this skill to help you make the right tradeoffs for progress. If you have the other four skills, these resources will be helpful, but without the other four, making tradeoffs becomes very difficult.

MAKING IT REAL

Once again, let's compare young Bob with enlightened Bob.

5. MAKING TRADE-OFFS

1 ◄──────────────────► 10
YOUNG BOB   ENLIGHTENED BOB

Young Bob doesn't believe in tradeoffs. As a result, I am always trying to reach all the requirements all the time—to make something everybody wants. But it's never good enough, never fast enough, never cheap enough. In the end, I always view my work as suboptimal because it can always be better if I only had more time and money. When I ultimately run out of time and money, the tradeoffs just happen to my thing.

Enlightened Bob, on the other hand, tries to understand the tradeoffs that result from demand and considers this a key input early in development. I value the time it takes to develop something and look at the unknowns to manage risk. I realize that nothing will be perfect. As a result, enlightened Bob ends up with a kick-ass half that takes off; meanwhile, young Bob gets a half-assed whole that has everything but does nothing well.

In the end, you're looking for balance between quality, cost, and time. Think better, faster, cheaper. You can have two but never all three. Here are a few steps that you can take to start practicing the skills taught in this chapter:

- Look at a problem that you're trying to solve. Where do you feel like you're chasing your tail—solving one problem only to create another? Now take a step back and explicitly identify the tradeoffs that you could make to solve the problem. What problems are and aren't acceptable?

- Go back to the hypothetical questions that I detailed above and ask yourself those same questions. For example, if I had to go faster, what would I change? If I had more money, what would I do differently? Now, are the decisions that you're making in alignment with your priorities? What levers can you pull to frame your situation better?

Here are some resources to help continue your education into making tradeoffs:

- *Total Design: Integrated Methods for Successful Product Engineering* by Stuart Pugh

- *Management for Quality Improvement: The 7 New QC Tools* by Sigeru Mizuno

- *Getting Started with Conjoint Analysis: Strategies for Product Design and Pricing Research* by Bryan K. Orme

- *Tolerance Design: A Handbook for Developing Optimal Specifications* by Clyde Creveling

- *Uncommon Service: How to Win by Putting Customers at the Core of Your Business* by Frances Frei and Anne Morriss

- *The Innovator's Dilemma: When New Technologies Cause Great Firms to Fail* by Clayton Christensen

- *Getting Real: The Smarter, Faster, Easier Way to Build a Successful Web Application* by Jason Fried, David Heinemeier Hansson, and Matthew Linderman

By now, you can probably see how the five skills of innovators and entrepreneurs fit together. The most skilled innovators and entrepreneurs I've met along the way have the ability to weave all five skills together. Let's take a step back and look at the whole.

PART THREE

PUTTING IT TOGETHER AND HELPING YOU MAKE PROGRESS

CHAPTER SEVEN

INTEGRATING THE FIVE SKILLS

These five skills are not for the masses: it's going to be hard. I believe there's not one predictable way to innovate, but these skills are a method for building a reliable process for how to think in virtually any situation. No one of these skills in isolation will make you a great innovator or entrepreneur; the challenge lies in applying all five. They're interdependent. For the book, I've just artificially separated them. In fact, you're better off doing a half-assed job at all five than being excellent at any one of these skills. It's not about the parts. It's about the whole.

As a young engineer, I didn't understand that, so when I started to realize some of these skills, like prototyping, I became obsessed; I wanted to teach everyone. "Let me show you how I solved this problem," I would say after my first successful prototype, solving the paint problem in cars. As my process evolved, I realized that successful innovators and entrepreneurs understood empathetic perspective, uncovering demand, causal structures, prototyping to learn, and making tradeoffs. It wasn't about any single skill.

The Natural Priority

There's a natural priority to mastering the five skills of innovators and entrepreneurs. Let's look at how each of the five skills help each other. I determine the natural priority whenever I'm given a list of tasks to accomplish. Draw a circle with arrows that show the other tasks on the list that each skill assists with. Now you have the natural priority of how to move through the work.

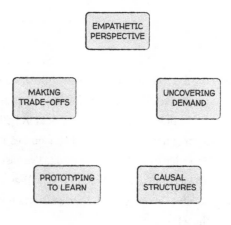

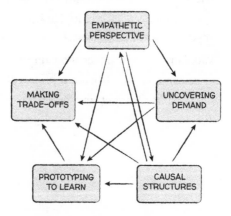

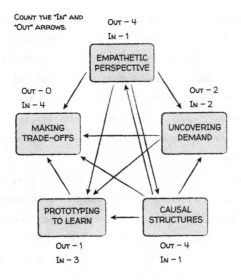

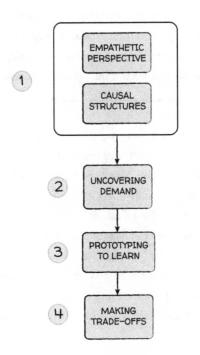

Look at the five skills of innovators and entrepreneurs, for instance. I've drawn a circle that demonstrates how each skill helps with another. As you can see, empathetic perspective and causal structures both help with every other skill. Meanwhile, uncovering demand only helps prototyping to learn and making tradeoffs. Prototyping to learn only helps making tradeoffs. Finally, mastering making tradeoffs does not help any of the other four skills.

Knowing this natural priority will help you work through the task. I often find myself being asked to assist someone in making tradeoffs, but the truth is that those tradeoffs don't happen in a vacuum; I must take a step back and work the other four skills before I can help. There's a natural sequence for how things are built, and this is the tool that I use to understand the interdependence.

It's natural to assume that they are independent skills that you work through off a list, but when you get to work, you will find that uncovering demand, for instance, is way easier if you have empathetic perspective and causal structures.

When people come to me, they usually don't really want to know *how* to solve the problem; they just want the problem solved. But out of the thousands, there are hundreds who ask, "How did you do that?" with genuine interest. This book is for them. It's not a simple conversation where I can sit down and teach them prototyping, and suddenly, they can change the world. It's a complex, layered process that takes time and practice. Sometimes the easiest way to understand the complex is to make it simple, so let's first tie it all together by making dinner using the five skills of innovators and entrepreneurs, then I'll show you how I used it to write this book.

APPLYING THE FIVE SKILLS TO LIFE

There are numerous mundane tasks in everyday life where you already use the five skills of innovators and entrepreneurs without even realizing it. My goal is to make that explicit so that you start to become more conscious and take it to the next level. Take dinner, for instance: it's something you produce every day, and without even realizing it, you're utilizing the five skills.

Most of the time, dinner starts the week before, right? You need to go grocery shopping, so you think about the meals that you'll want to make for that week and the ingredients that you'll need.

As you do so, you're thinking about the context for each meal: who are you feeding—spouse, kids, company? You are looking into the future and deciding if you'll be busy that day and need a quick meal that gets the job done, or something more elaborate. What meal did you have the night before? After all, you want variety, not chicken five nights in a row. This planning, where you unpack the context for dinner, is *uncovering demand*.

As you're planning, you are also thinking about everybody else. What kid's going to complain? Are there allergies to contend with? Maybe you decide to accept not satisfying one of the kids to make the dinner that you want. Or maybe you strive to please everyone, and therefore, you're willing to make something everyone will eat but no one will really love. You're *making tradeoffs* that you're identifying through *empathetic perspective* as you go through the process of planning dinner.

Next, you need to figure out how you're going to cook the meal. Do you need a side dish—salad or vegetable? What about dessert? Is there an appetizer because there's a football game on? How many things are you going to serve? What sequence do you need to cook them in? Does dinner need to start at a certain time? When do you need to start cooking? That's *causal structures*.

Wrapped within causal structures is the notion of *prototyping to learn*. Maybe you need to cook one thing faster to make room in the oven. If you cook it at a hotter temperature, it'll be done faster, but the meat might be drier. What's more important? So you start *making tradeoffs.* Maybe you're missing an ingredient. Do you send someone to the store, which would delay dinner, or make a substitution? You are prototyping the best way to cook dinner while managing tradeoffs because you are playing out the consequence of each decision.

As you cook dinner every night, you are practicing the five skills of innovators and entrepreneurs simultaneously. You make decisions through this unconscious process. You are deciding what progress means for you as the cook versus the people eating. And it all plays a role in designing dinner. These are the skills that you need to cultivate to be a successful innovator and entrepreneur.

Now let's unpack the five skills in a more complex setting: how I wrote this book.

APPLYING THE FIVE SKILLS TO INNOVATION

I hired Scribe Media to help me write this book, and they have a process that they detail for you at the start of the journey. It's the steps involved in writing the book from the beginning to the end, laid out in a brochure: manuscript interviews, manuscript writing, cover design, editing, etc. Most people would look at this journey and think that the work is the process, the steps, but that's more of a task list, telling you how you'll get there. The process itself tells you nothing about the experience of innovating as an author. Think of it as macro level versus micro level. The steps are at the macro level, but the real work happens at the micro level, where the five skills become critical.

EMPATHETIC PERSPECTIVE

EMPATHETIC PERSPECTIVE

PEOPLE WITH THIS SKILL CAN DETACH FROM THEIR OWN PERSPECTIVE AND SEE THE SUBTLE DIFFERENCES BETWEEN THE MANY DIFFERENT PERSPECTIVES SURROUNDING THEIR THING—INTERNALLY AND EXTERNALLY

As an innovator, I needed to recognize the many different perspectives involved in creating my book: the reader, myself (the author), the scribe, the cover designer, the editor, the project manager, promotions, Amazon, etc. Empathetic perspective is understanding the people and things that were wrapped around my ability to produce the book.

Now Scribe Media would manage those relationships for me, but I still needed to have an empathetic perspective, particularly as it related to the critical roles: the reader, myself, and my scribe. My scribe and I needed to be aligned to create a successful book. Don't get me wrong. Scribe Media has a great process for book writing, but it's not their process that makes it all work; it's the interaction between myself and my scribe and how we'd collaborate on the common vision for the reader that would make the difference.

For instance, when I'd talk through the content, I'd recognize that it was new to my scribe. For her to write it well, she'd need to truly grasp the material. And so I'd try to teach her so that she could teach the reader. She wasn't my assistant, regurgitating the material; she was the one who would design the reader's experience. Because of that, I'd usually provide five examples where the reader may only need three. Then I wasn't dictating which examples she'd use. I'd leave it to her to make those tradeoffs. I wasn't trying to prescribe the solution; I was giving her the latitude to pick the stories that would work best and design the experience for the reader. My dyslexia may have actually been an advantage in this situation because I knew I couldn't write the book, so I'd leave it to the expert. But therefore, I needed an empathetic perspective toward my scribe.

To that end, on the welcome call, we talked about my workload. At the time, I was just launching *Demand-Side Sales 101*, and we discussed my priorities, but I wanted to understand her situation as well: How many other books was she working on? What types of deadlines did she have? This helped me identify tradeoffs from both of our perspectives. I knew that I'd rather push the book's publication date out than sacrifice quality. I didn't want her to rush writing it at the same time she was writing another manuscript. I'd rather space our calls so that my book would land at an ideal time for her to write.

Most people believe that it's the process that makes something work, but really, it's these micro behaviors that have the biggest impact. It's the freedom for her to do what she is good at and me to do what I am good at. She wouldn't ask me to spell and I wouldn't ask her to engineer something. We'd remain sensitive to each other's strengths and weaknesses, as well as the kind of energy it'd take to write a great book.

UNCOVERING DEMAND

UNCOVERING DEMAND
PEOPLE WITH THIS SKILL CAN DETACH FROM THEIR PRODUCT OR SERVICE AND LOOK AT THE DEMAND-SIDE OF THE EQUATION—SEEING STRUGGLES, CONTEXT, AND OUTCOMES.

But before my scribe and I could take all of my ideas, knowledge, and content and put it into the book, we needed to think about the reader. That started with uncovering demand: the who, when, where, and why somebody would pick up this book and fit it into their lives. What are the struggling moments people have wrapped around this book? What are the outcomes that this book would help them achieve? And then what other books, classes, etc. might do the same "job-"?

So we built a set of JTBD based off **real** people who've come to me over the years struggling with innovation and wanting help—a "job" story that represented many real, struggling moments—as part of Scribe Media's document called the North Star.

JTBD #1

JTBD #2

JTBD #3

JTBD #4

Our "job" story started with Mary, who is the head of an innovation group at her company. She has a ton of money and a lot of responsibility and freedom to go build products, but she's had little success. Mary knows the mechanics of product development; she's followed the rules and processes from an academic perspective, but she cannot figure out the missing ingredient. She feels like she did not do anything wrong yet is still failing.

I know from talking to people that many resonate with this experience. They keep putting more and more money into innovation, but they are not getting any return on the investment, and they cannot figure out why. They keep expecting the process to fix their innovation problem, but they haven't invested in any of the skills. It's not hard to see the forces at play.

- **Pushes:** when we've been trying to do something, and it hasn't worked; when we've gone through all the right steps, but we haven't gotten the results; when my team is not working on the right things; when we feel like we are spinning our wheels.

- **Pulls:** help me read a book so I can reframe my problem; so I can change the way that we think about things; so I can modify our process and launch good innovations; so my team can have a common language; so we can build frameworks that take us to the next level.

Those real, struggling moments lead people to seek help, oftentimes through a consultant like myself. And while that fixes the problem in the moment, it does not help them really develop the skills internally that they need to be successful the next time. People end up replicating the same behavior as opposed to understanding the underlying skills needed for success. I wanted this book to be the "a-ha" moment: "I've been looking at all the wrong things; I've been looking at the symptoms, but I never understood the underlying causal reasons of what I needed to do differently."

Before we started talking about the book's content, we framed demand from the buyer/reader part of the world—the context that they are in, and the outcomes that they seek. I think of it as drilling down into that box so that I can understand the different cases of why readers would pick up this book. We also considered the fact that in some cases, the buyer and the reader are different people: companies to employees, professors to students. We did not build the book and then search for an audience but rather uncovered demand and then built the book.

CAUSAL STRUCTURES

CAUSAL STRUCTURES
PEOPLE WITH THIS SKILL HAVE A DOMINANT
VIEW OF HOW THE WORLD WORKS BASED IN
CAUSE AND EFFECT.

Once I knew the customer and understood the things wrapped around my book, we had to slow things way down, take a step back, and look at the whole so we could design a process for the reader. We had a pile of components, like a complex jigsaw puzzle, that we basically dumped on the table and said, "Okay, here it is. How are we going to pull it all together so it's logical for the reader?" This was all about the cause-and-effect structure of the book.

- An introduction and conclusion

- The five skills: empathetic perspective, uncovering demand, causal structures, prototyping to learn, and making tradeoffs

- My four mentors: Drs. Genichi Taguchi, W. Edwards Deming, Willie Moore, and Clayton Christensen

- The concept of young Bob versus enlightened Bob

- A compilation of stories

- Content that we needed to teach

Ultimately, we built a system that became the chapters of the book, with the readers' outcomes in mind. Causal structures are the ability to see all of that and make sense of the pieces in a way that designs a path to the outcomes you seek. It's the notion of being able to bucket things and then figure out how to build to get the desired outcomes. When we meet the outcomes, we are really meeting demand. Causal structures are about getting from the mess into a linear process. It's about understanding how things work and how they connect to each other. Scribe Media calls this portion the "roadmap"—I think of it as more of a guide than a real roadmap because of all the unknowns and tradeoffs ahead.

PROTOTYPING TO LEARN

PROTOTYPING TO LEARN
PEOPLE WITH THIS SKILL KNOW THAT THEY DO NOT HAVE ALL THE ANSWERS AND RUN TESTS TO GET EMPIRICAL DATA TO DISCOVER AND BUILD NEW THEORY INSTEAD OF RELYING ON EXISTING THEORY AND TESTING HYPOTHESES.

Once we saw the whole, we needed to play with how we were going to lay it out in the book. That's prototyping. For instance, the five skills are so intertwined, but we needed to separate them and develop the most logical sequence for the reader. How did each skill build on the next? How did they help each other? How could we make sure they were modular enough? What stories would teach which content the best? In fact, we went back and forth a bit about whether we should have *uncovering demand* or *empathetic perspective* first.

Then we needed to layer in my mentors in a logical, digestible manner, but each of them taught me multiple skills, so where would they go? We talked about delving into each of them in the Introduction or Chapter 1, but that bogged down the pace too much for the reader. We played with putting one mentor within each chapter, but they each taught me multiple skills; plus, we had five skills and four mentors. Then we talked about creating an appendix of my mentors. Ultimately, we decided that dividing up their stories would be more interesting than the back-to-back pace the appendix would create, so we developed chapter interludes and included additional stories within the chapters where they naturally fit the content. We proto-typed by playing with the sequence of events.

MAKING TRADEOFFS

MAKING TRADE–OFFS
PEOPLE WITH THIS SKILL UNDERSTAND
THAT THEY CANNOT DO EVERYTHING AND
ARE SKILLED AT MAKING ESSENTIAL
TRADE–OFFS TO LAUNCH A PRODUCT THAT
IS NOT PERFECT.

Ultimately, we had to make tradeoffs about what to include and what to leave out. And part of that was recognizing the amount of progress a book can make versus the consulting I traditionally do. I could see there was a gap between what I wanted to give the reader and what was possible. You can't fit twenty pounds of crap into a five-pound bag. I needed to make tradeoffs: "You're better off with a kick-ass half than a half-assed whole." So we recognized that the book would be more about getting people started than helping everybody become an expert. Our goal was to create a jumping-off point that would take the reader from level ten to a twenty-five, or level thirty to fifty, but we did not expect the book to take anyone to one hundred.

Scribe Media's process created a set of constraints that forced us to stay within those limits. We interviewed for the Introduction first, even though it's the hardest chapter. Initially, I felt like it would be so much easier to do it last and struggled to zero in on the "right" level of material. It actually took us two calls to interview for that section instead of the typical one call. My scribe and I talked at length about how introductions are always the hardest part. She told me that they are the hardest part of the book to write; they always take her at least twice as long as any other chapter. Why not do the Introduction last? She and I mentally prototyped that question.

We both concluded that producing the Introduction first, while hard, served a larger purpose. It would set the entire framework for the book, which would give us boundaries. These boundaries could help us make tradeoffs as we went through the rest of the manuscript: what was in and what was out. Doing the hard work first would make everything else easier. And when you think about it, constraints also make good economic sense because without them, the book could go on forever. The constraint shows you when you've gone too far.

The work of the book was also broken into parts. We interviewed from September through December, but I knew that once those calls ended, the content would be locked, so it forced me to prototype in that time box. These constraints forced me to say, "Here's what I can put in, and here's where I've got to make a tradeoff." And without those constraints, I guarantee the book would be no better, there would actually be more risk that it would be worse.

HOW THE FIVE SKILLS MAKE LIFE BETTER

It doesn't matter if you're trying to make dinner, write a book, or even buy a house. These five skills are at the core of making life better. Yet they are the things that are in between, that no one seems to talk about. Most people consider this the "art" of innovation. The reason that these skills are so elusive is precisely because they are so intertwined; they happen so quickly that people don't even recognize them as separate things. But when you separate the five skills and make them explicit, they enable you to take everything to the next level.

There's not one skill that's more important than another, but different circumstances may draw more on one skill than another. For instance, if you're a salesperson, empathetic perspective is even more important. Additionally, some of these skills build on each other: Empathetic perspective is the thing that allows you to see demand, helps you manage tradeoffs and see the causal structures, and therefore, prototype to learn. If you do not have empathetic perspective, it's nearly impossible to master any of the other skills because they build upon it. Causal structures are the other skill that's critical to master before you'll be able to achieve success with the rest. If you're weak in empathetic perspective and causal structures, you end up weak in the others as well. Those two are the most foundational of the five skills.

Overall, I see these skills not just as the key to innovation and entrepreneurship but as the foundational skills to a happy life. They help you make progress; they help you help others make progress, which in turn makes you happy. Life is about a series of tradeoffs that you make, not the magic of getting it all. No one has everything.

CONCLUSION

"I'm trying to free your mind...But I can only show you the door. You're the one that has to walk through it."

—**Morpheus**, fictional character, *The Matrix*

The simplest thing you can do at this point is close the book. You're done, right? The problem: you can't unsee it; it's powerful stuff. This book is the red pill of innovation, and now that you've consumed it, you won't look at innovation and entrepreneurship the same. You're like me—prone to overthinking—I'm sorry. But I believe that the world would be better off if more of us overthought life. Imagine the impact on society as a whole. Hopefully, I've inspired you to take the five skills to the next level. So what next? Ask yourself the following questions:

- What struggle did this book reveal to me, and what progress do I want to make because I read this book?

- What did I hire this book to do?

I've categorized the reasons that people would hire this book into four JTBD categories:

1. **Help me extend myself so I can better myself.** I am a lifelong learner. Reading this book was more of a personal quest to better myself and learn new skills. While I'm

interested, I don't need to apply this material in an accountable way. It's similar to a hobby, like gardening or learning to play chess. Progress for this "job" is about ongoing, continuous self-improvement.

2. **Help me take a deep dive into areas where I'm lacking so that I can improve the way I design and innovate.** I'm a builder/creator of things. Reading this book opened my eyes to my strengths and weaknesses. I can see now where I excel and where I need to improve to take my innovations to the next level. There's work that I need to do, but I'm approaching it as an individual.

3. **Help me add these skills to my organization so that my teams can successfully innovate.** I run an organization. Reading this book showed me that as an organization, we need to work on developing these skills. We have the tools and the processes to innovate, but we are missing the ingredients in between; I can see that we are not clicking on all cylinders.

4. **Help me learn these skills so that I can run my small business more successfully.** We are not in the business of innovation, but reading this book showed me that learning to flex these innovation muscles could help me respond better to changing markets and help me advance my small business.

Now let's take a deep dive into each of the four JTBD, and I'll outline what's next for taking the five skills to the next level.

JTBD ONE

Jay is a lifelong learner. He's one of those people who picks up every self-improvement or productivity book because he's always trying to better himself. He's looking for that one nugget that's going to help him be better. He's not trying to tell anybody about it; he's not reading it for anybody else. It's about self-improvement. This book showed Jay where he could work on strengthening his skills. What next?

I recommend Jay start by picking one of the skills, not all five at once. You need to master each separately before practicing them collectively. It's like swimming: I'm going to teach you arms, breathing, and kicking first, but separately; only then are we going to pull it all together in the pool. Once you pick a skill to practice, I want you to find an everyday situation where you can apply it. Take gardening, for example. Let's plan a garden and zero in on the skill that needs honing.

- **Empathetic Perspective:** Look at the entire journey of planting a vegetable garden. What are the many different perspectives wrapped around the garden? Think of everything from the resources you have, such as space, sunlight, etc.? Almost become the seed, and say, "Can I really grow here?" Say it's tomato plants. How big will they get? Will the birds and squirrels eat them? What vegetables are you going to eat? What are you going to make with the vegetables?

- **Uncovering Demand:** What is the progress that you want to make by having a garden? What are the outcomes you seek? Is it about having farm-to-table fresh food? Maybe you want to donate your vegetables? Or is it about the pride of growing something from nothing?

- **Causal Structures:** Let's think about the components involved in planting a garden. How much dirt do you need? How much water? How much space does everything need? What's the portfolio of things that you can actually put in there?

- **Prototyping to Learn:** Think about your garden throughout the year. What are you going to plant this season versus
  next season? How will the fertilizer or the watering change?
  Start to think through how you will play with all of these
  different parameters.

- **Making Tradeoffs:** How much space does something take?
  How long does it take to grow? For instance, lettuce grows
  faster and will keep growing over time, whereas potatoes
  take up a lot of space. What's the yield you really want?
  How do you frame the tradeoffs? How do you continuously
  improve season to season?

You don't have to apply this to gardening. You could apply it to
planning a vacation, buying a car, volunteering at church, etc. The
key is to practice the skills one at a time in an everyday scenario and
learn how to take it to the next level.

JTBD TWO

Justin is a software entrepreneur. He's been building products for
a while, but he recognizes that he's not perfect. He reads books to
help him round out his perspective and grow individually so that
he can build better products. While reading this book, he has identified two of the five skills where he feels he needs to better himself.
What next?

I recommend that Justin start with a postmortem. A postmortem is a way to look back at a recent project and conduct somewhat
of a JTBD interview where you unpack what happened and why it
happened. I do this exact thing when consulting; here's how I walk
people through the process:

- **Warmup:** What was the best part of the project? What was the worst part of the project?

- **Timeline:** Draw the project in pictures, no words, from start to finish. What was the sequence of events? What dominoes fell along the way? This is about getting you to remember what happened.

- **Label Events:** Then I have them go through the drawn timeline and place letters (F, W, H, U, R, P) that indicated their feelings in each stage. Where were you frustrated (F)? Where did the road wash out (W)? Where did you get help (H)? Where were you unsure (U)? Where did you resent an action that you took (R)? Where did you get pushed onto a path that you didn't want to take (P)? You're trying to overlay the emotional and social aspects of the project.

- **Talk:** Now it's time to discuss the drawing. And ultimately, the goal is to be able to understand what you learned. If you could go back and take the red pill of innovation before this project, what would you do differently that would have the greatest impact? What actions would you start, stop, or continue?

PROJECT POST MORTEM

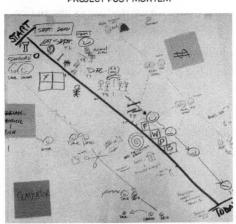

$$F = \underline{F}rustration$$
$$W = Road \ \underline{WASHED} \ OUT$$
$$H = Got \ \underline{H}elp$$
$$B = Took \ a \ step \ \underline{BACK}$$
$$U = UNSure \ wHAT \ to \ Do \ Next$$
$$P = Got \ \underline{P}ush \ Down \ a \ Path \ We \ DIDN'T \ WANT$$

By looking backwards in this way, you can then project forward to the next project and know *where* and *when* you need to apply the five skills, not just how to do the skill. Now look forward two or three weeks. How can you inject these skills into your current project? I call this reflective learning. If you only look forward, you're likely to continue to strengthen the skills that you're already good at, rather than work on your weaknesses.

JTBD THREE

Susan's a leader who runs a department and has a team that she's responsible for. She may have started reading the book with "Job One" or "Job Two" in mind, but after its conclusion, she realizes that she needs to build these skills within her team. They excel with processes and tools, but she can see some of the gaps in the five skills. What next?

In this scenario, I recommend starting with a *Learning to Build* book club for the cross-functional team. Then once everyone understands the five skills, I'd do a postmortem—as described in "Job Two"—for your most recent innovation. What skills are you the weakest in? Where do you excel? Now prioritize the weak skills for overall improvement. To start, assign one person to the job of mastering each of the skills where you are weak. For example, it's somebody's job to do a deep dive into prototyping to learn and someone else's job to investigate empathetic perspective. Then once a week, carve out two to three hours of project time to discuss how the team will apply the skills to the timeline for the current project.

JTBD FOUR

Ashley is running a small business, say an accounting organization, that's been around for twenty years. They've been doing their tasks the same way forever. After reading this book, she realizes that they've been reacting to changes rather than being proactive. She realizes that they need to innovate, but they don't have any of the skills. She wants to use the book to introduce everyone to some new ideas so that they can figure out how to evolve better.

I recommend that they first take a deep dive into uncovering demand. There are two good signs to look for when identifying a struggling moment:

1. **Nonconsumption:** Where do people want to make progress, but they can't? You see this where people keep complaining but don't act. They want to do something; they want to reach for something, but they either don't feel they can, or they don't feel that it's possible. For example, nobody spends time finding a better bank because they think banks are all the same. Find the places where people are complacent, so they're just accepting inferiority.

2. **Work-arounds:** Figure out where people are doing work-arounds? For example, "I export this, I put that here, then I do this…" They have five extra steps for getting something done that should be possible to streamline. Those are struggling moments. Where are the work-arounds in your business?

Once you've uncovered demand through identifying the struggling moments, either internally or externally, start applying the five skills of innovators and entrepreneurs to two of the struggles.

- **Empathetic Perspective:** what are the different perspectives wrapped around that struggling moment?

- **Causal Structures:** What's the cause-and-effect relationship behind the struggling moment? What's not happening? Or what's happening that should not be happening?

- **Prototyping to Learn:** how can I play with the system to help people make progress?

- **Managing Tradeoffs:** what are the tradeoffs that I can make to improve the struggling moment?

LAST THOUGHTS...

"The only metrics that will truly matter to my life are the individuals whom I have been able to help, one by one, to become better people."

—Clayton Christensen, *How Will You Measure Your Life*

Innovation and entrepreneurship are entirely about helping people make progress. That's the purpose of this book—to pass forward the lessons taught to me by giants in innovation and entrepreneurship so that you can make progress and in turn help others.

I recognize that this book may cause you to have more questions than answers; it's a jumping-off point for digging deeper. Are you ready? It's not going to be easy, but it'll be worth it. Once you pull together the fundamental pieces, it will spin you up in a way that allows you to see the world nobody else can see—*The Matrix*. You will swallow the red pill of innovation and become more choiceful and thoughtful, and in turn, you will have the power to change the world.

Now go make progress! Learn to build!

I hope this book has helped you be a better person. If so, please let me know on LinkedIn—Bob Moesta. Thanks!

ABOUT THE AUTHOR

Bob Moesta is one of the principal architects of the Jobs to Be Done theory and founder of The Re-Wired Group. Since developing the Jobs to Be Done theory in the mid-90s along with Harvard Business School Professor Clayton Christensen, Bob has continued to develop, advance, and apply the innovation framework to everyday business challenges.

A visual thinker, teacher, and creator, Bob has worked on and helped launch more than thirty-five hundred new products, services, and businesses across nearly every industry, including defense, automotive, software, financial services, and education, among many others. He has started, built, and sold several startups.

Bob is an entrepreneur at heart and engineer and designer by training. He started out as an intern for Dr. W. Edwards Deming, father of the quality revolution, and worked with Dr. Genichi Taguchi extensively. In Japan, Bob learned firsthand many of the lean product development methods for which so many Japanese businesses, including Toyota, are known.

A lifetime learner, Bob holds a degree from Michigan State University in electrical engineering. He has studied extensively at Harvard Business School, Stanford University, Boston University's Questrom School of Business, and at MIT School of Engineering. He is a fellow at the Clayton Christensen Institute and is a guest lecturer at Harvard Business School, MIT's Sloan School of Management, and Northwestern University's Kellogg School of Management.

ACKNOWLEDGMENTS

Writing a book is a huge undertaking that is not done alone, though there is usually only one author. This book, like my previous books, is a culmination of so many of my life experiences, collaborations, and research done with others. It is impossible for me to acknowledge everyone who has contributed to me, my life, and this book over my years. I have received so much help as a dyslexic kid from Detroit. I am thankful to so many people, too many to list everyone, but you know who you are, and I am blessed, thankful, and truly appreciative of all the help throughout the years. THANK YOU!

That said, I have a few very specific people who helped me directly on this book.

I want to thank Greg Engle for being my business partner for almost two decades. We make a great team. We talk through everything together.

I want to thank my family. Family is the core of everything for me, and this book would not be possible without them. To my wife Julie, for all her encouragement, and our kids Marty, Mary, Henry, and Susie, as well as my brothers Bill, Alan, and Greg, and my sisters Sue, Jane and Patrice, thank you for creating an environment that enabled me to write this book. To my late Mom and saint, Mary, who was endlessly patient. I had way too much energy, and she channeled it in a way that enabled me to become more than a baggage handler at a metro airport, which was the result of my high school occupational test.

I want to thank the many mentors who have guided me throughout the years, starting with my four core mentors, Dr. W. Edwards Deming, Dr. Clayton Christensen, Dr. Genichi Taguchi, and Dr. Willie Moore, then additionally, Shin Taguchi, Yuin Wu, Yoji Akao, Dr. Don Clausing, Larry Sullivan, David Lord, Steve Ungvari, Alan Wu, Jim Wilkensen, Tim Davis, Martin Dierkes, Jason Fried, Ryan Singer, Michael Horn, Ethan Bernstein, David Schonthal, Derek Van Bever, John Palmer, and Rick Pedi.

To my coworkers at The Re-Wired Group and the people who I've worked with throughout the years, especially Greg Engle, Chris Spiek, Katherine Thompson, Matt Sheppard, Ervin Fowlkes, Lauren Lackey, Bob Barrett, Brian Tolle, and Alan Lowenthal: thank you.

I also want to thank the people from Scribe Media who worked on this book, especially Janet Murnaghan, Barbara Boyd, Emily Anderson, Jericho Westendorf, Neddie Ann Underwood, Zach Obront, and Tucker Max. And the people who read the book in advance and offered feedback: Julie Moesta, Greg Engle, Katherine Thompson, Ryan Singer, Michael Horn, Des Traynor, Jason Scully, Andy Weisbecker, Rusty Zaspel, Bill Aulet, Todd Rose, David Schonthal, Craig Wortmann, Peter Muir, Mike Belsito, Paul McAvinchey, Lauren Lackey, Jay Gerhart. A special thank you to Des Traynor for writing the Foreword to the book. And thanks to Amrita Gurney for allowing us to include an excerpt of her Peloton interview.

This book is a combination of life experiences; there were so many people involved. These acknowledgments are the 20 percent that represents the 80 percent of all the people who have helped me. Thank you!

Printed in the USA
CPSIA information can be obtained
at www.ICGtesting.com
LVHW091147090923
757725LV00012B/59/J